African-American Managers' Perceptions About Factors That Impact Their Career Development & Job Opportunities

by

Glenn H. Walton, Ph.D.

authorHOUSE®

AuthorHouse™
1663 Liberty Drive, Suite 200
Bloomington, IN 47403
www.authorhouse.com
Phone: 1-800-839-8640

First published by AuthorHouse 11/4/2008

ISBN: 978-1-4343-2281-4 (sc)

Library of Congress Control Number: 2007931777

Printed in the United States of America
Bloomington, Indiana

This book is printed on acid-free paper.

I dedicate this dissertation to some special persons who are very significant to me, my family. Alice and the late Lee Henry Walton, mother and father, who were very supportive while I was pursuing this doctoral degree. I also dedicate it to my grandmother tho planted the seed of education which was developed in my life over the years.

Acknowledgements

The writer wishes to express appreciation to the members of his Doctoral Dissertation Committee: Dr. Evelyn Ortiz, Faculty Advisor; Dr. Robert S. Butters, Faculty Reader; and Dr. Maria A. Irizarry, External Consultant for their advice and support in the realization of this study. He is also pleased by all the African-American Managers who collaborated by answering the questionnaire and by the Springfield Urban League, Illinois African-American Businesses, Illinois Central Management Services, and Walton Management and Associates, Incorporated, that made the study possible. He is grateful to the Black American Associations for the information and materials that urged him to participate in the research activity. Special mention should be made of the generous help of his brothers and sisters: Hane, Charles, Henry, Jr., Reginald N., Ronnie, Annie L., Augusta, Barbara J., Bertha and his dearest children: Bernadette, Gregory, Glenn, Jr., Nancy N., Marlin and Marlene. He also wishes to thank those families whose names he might have overlooked for their support.

Table of Contents

Chapter 1 Introduction 1

Statement of the Problem 2

Purpose of the Study..3

Significance of the Study 3

Research Questions...3

Assumptions of the Study 4

Limitations of the Study...4

Definition of Terms 4

Chapter 2 Review Literature 7

Introduction..7

The Historical Background of Perceptions 7

Perceptions 9

Nineteenth Century: Trade...11

The Changing Environment..12

Government Legislation..12

Managerial Styles...13

African-American Managers: Leaders and Managers.......................14

African-American Business Managers 17

Organizational Structure and the Need of Black Administrators.......18

Administrative "Culture" and the African-American Manager 18

Organizational Directors and Black Administrative Outlook............19

African-American Managers' Work Force and Competition.............21

Personnel Selection 22

Conclusions 25

Chapter 3 Methodology 27

Design of the Study..27

Definition of Variables 27

Description of the Population and Sample 28

Description of the Instrument 28

Validation and Reliability of the Instrument....................................29

Research Procedure...29

Procedure for Statistical Analysis 30

Chapter4 Presentation and Analysis of Data..33

Socio Demographic Profile of the Sample 33

Working Experience..33

Level of Education 34

Affirmative Actions Programs..34

Position...34

Research Questions...35

Chapter5 Conclusions, Implications and Recommendations **55**

    Conclusions 55

    Implications..55

    Recommendations...57

Bibliography **59**

Appendix...**63**

List of Tables

Table 1: Descriptive Statistics for Gender 33

Table 2: Descriptive Statistics for Years of Experience 34

Table 3: Summary Statistics for Level of Education 34

Table 4: Summary Statistics for Affirmative Action Programs 34

Table 5: Summary Statistics for Position Held 35

Table 6: Cross Tabulation of Type Organization by Perceptions Academic Qualification Required 35

Table 7: Cross Tabulation of Type of Organization by Perception of Academic Preparation Required 36

Table 8: Cross Tabulation of Type of Organization by Preference of Type of Candidates...36

Table 9: Cross Tabulation of Type of Organization by Perception of Previous Jobs as Source of Experience in Management 37

Table 10: Cross tabulation of Type of Organization by Perception of Limited Experience in Management 38

Table 11: Cross tabulation of Type of Organization by AAM Participation in Professional Network 38

Table 12: Cross Tabulation of Type of Organization by Degree of Agreement in Inappropriate Professional Networking 39

Table 13: Cross tabulation and Chi-Square Analysis of Managers with Affirmative Action Programs vs Those Without Those Programs Regarding Qualification (Item 6) 40

Table 14: Cross Tabulation of Managers with Affirmative Action Programs vs Those Without Those Programs Regarding Other Attributes (Item 7) 40

Table 15: Cross Tabulation of Managers with Affirmative Actions Programs vs Those Without Those Programs Regarding Experience in Previous Jobs (Item 9)...................41

Table 16: Cross Tabulation of Managers with Affirmative Action Programs vs. Those Without Those Programs Regarding In House Training (Item 10)...............................42

Table 17: Cross Tabulation Analysis of Managers with Affirmative Action Programs vs. Those Without Those Program Regarding Limited Experience for Managerial Position (Item 24)..42

Table 18: Cross Tabulation of Managers with Affirmative Action Programs vs Those Without those Programs Regarding Experienced AAM Interested in Managerial Positions at Time of Recruitment (Item 25)...43

Table 19: Cross Tabulation of Managers with Affirmative Action Programs vs. Those Without Those Programs Regarding Networking (Item 11).....................................43

Table 20: Cross Tabulation of Managers with Affirmative Action Programs vs. Those Without Those Programs Regarding Inappropriate Professional Networking Hindering Access to Managerial Position (Item 17)..44

Table 21: Cross Tabulation of Managers with Affirmative Action Programs vs. Those Without Those Program Regarding Job Opportunities (Item 19)...............................44

Table 22: Cross Tabulation of Type of Organization by WM Preference of Management Styles (Item 28)..45

Table 23: Cross Tabulation Type of Organizations by AAM Preference of Management Styles (Item 29)..46

Table 24: Chi-Square Values for AAM's Career Development Indicators of Item 30..........46

Table 25: Cross Tabulation of Type of Organizationsby Lack of Confidence.....................47

Table 26: Cross Tabulation of Type of Organization by Lack of Discipline 47

Table 27: Cross Tabulation of Type of Organizationby Insufficient Education....................48

Table 28: Cross Tabulation of Type of Organizationby Lack of Technical and
Administrative Skills 48

Table 29: Cross tabulation of Type of Organization by Decision Making Styles................49

Table 30: Cross Tabulation of Type of Organizationby Lack of Time Management Skills..49

Table 31: Cross Tabulation of Type of Organizationby Lack of Experience........................50

Table 32: Cross Tabulation of Type of Organizationby Jealousy of AAM and Peers 50

Table 33: Cross Tabulation of Type of Organizationby AAM's Preference for Traditional
Roles 51

Table 34: Summary of Chi-Square Values forFactors Hindering AAM in Their Career
Development...51

Table 35: Cross Tabulation of Type of Organizationby Opinions of Managerial Styles 52

Table 36: Cross Tabulation of Type of Organization Preference (Item 37)..............................53

Table 37: Rank Ordering of Factors Affecting AAM Access to Managerial Positions 53

Chapter

1

Introduction

Toffler (1990) notes two imperatives in today's workplace. One is the "innovation imperative" in which creativity is paramount in a highly competitive world open to experimentation, liberation, and newness. The second "imperative is acceleration of response to change. Both forces are altering managerial practices as the "Third Wave," the information age, comes to be. As old power hierarchies of the past are eliminated, it becomes of special importance to discern how African-Americans may be expected to fare in an era driven by knowledge. It is evident that the top managers of the twenty-first century will need to master new techniques, adapt to new organizational forms, and create new ideas. Certainly no one population segment may be presumed more able to incorporate management driven by knowledge tenets. Yet, although overall intelligence between white and African-American aspirants to managerial ranks does not differ significantly, achieving those positions ± much lower for Black males and females. Members of the African-American Business Managers (AAM) find that one of the primary reasons restricting Black advancement are the perceptions of those in control of hiring and promoting personnel in the business world. Perceptions may best be defined as preconceived ideas that have been formed over time through formal and informal social interactions and cultural beliefs. Robbins (1991) finds that perception are in part determined by personal needs, interests, motives, expectations, and past experiences whether positive or negative in nature. Individuals may modify or distort the images perceived to more nearly conform to personal self-concept and understanding, forming a predetermined set of ideas about other people, situations, and structures. Perceptions may be held by top managers, predicated on these myriad factors, or by African-American managerial candidates aspiring to climb the administrative ladder. In both instances, perceptions too readily become a process of stereotyping.

It is perhaps simplistic to state that stereotypical patterns emerge only from the top (primarily white) managerial ranks. It is not difficult to ascribe false perceptions about African-American abilities, capabilities, work ethics, and creativity to lingering vestiges of racial prejudice. After all, more well-trained and well-prepared blacks are entering the work force each year seeking opportunities at those levels their education has opened to them. If not "wrong" perceptions, what influences those in control to pass over all too often these individuals for their white counterparts? Might there exist some reverse picture of perceptions, those held by African-American business personnel, that plays a role in the slow advancement of blacks to the more advantageous spots in corporations? Let us not, as it is said, blame the victim for his/her own fate, but rather call to examine in some depth the perceptions about African-Americans in the business world, about themselves, and how they might better those behavioral and psychological attributes mandatory if African-Americans are to be fully representative in the business climate of the twenty-first century.

STATEMENT OF THE PROBLEM

Raymond (1986) stipulates that in today's business organizations the emphasis is on flexibility, creativity, and the ability to compete. Ends, products, and outcomes are critical if the organization is to survive and prosper. Continual change and the ability to generate information on which informed change can occur cause about different ways of managing. Yet information is not simply knowledge exchanged among individuals and groups, but a vehicle for influencing and manipulating others, a route to creativity and transformation, to reform and renew for the organization as well as the individual.

In addressing the problems encountered by Black Americans, Garibaldi (1992) cites the factor that Black male students in particular are seldom challenged to succeed by their teachers. Those who do perform at or above average "are ostracized, ridiculed, intimidated, or belittled by peers". It may seem that academically talented individuals, those who might be expected to achieve in business, lack encouragement, positive feedback, and help in setting realistic goals. Therefore, from an early age, Blacks see negatives in striving and competing to get ahead" of their counterparts. Aggressiveness may cost them popularity if that drive is directed toward academics. Teachers, and often parents, do not believe in their abilities, lowering their self-esteem. Self-doubt and ambivalence about achievement are not what is demanded of today's management.

Another backdrop is created in the area of decision making. Prior, Thompson, and Miller (1991) find that people, especially minorities and women, are rarely taught formal strategies for solving problems and making decisions, two attributes required of management. Decisions may be made with no apparent rationale or consideration of possible consequences. "The results often reinforce the individual's beliefs that he/she cannot make decisions or that other more important people should do so" (p.34).

O'Sullivan and Baber (1991) point out the "multicultural" component of perceptions. Many Black aspirants have had limited experience with other populations. Previous intercultural exchanges may only extend to the college classroom or encounters in the workplace, and are casual at best. Some persons think they are competent "in multicultural knowledge, skills and attitudes but in actuality, have a long way to go. Others develop a genuine appreciation for some cultures but lack knowledge of, or do not feel comfortable with others" (p.13).. In the diverse workplace of the present, more training in multiculturalism is clearly indicated in order to avoid false perceptions which lead to failure to attain. O'Sullivan and Baber (1991) note that working with culturaly different people leads one to feel "nervous, anxious, inadequate, defensive, angry, uncomfortable, and incompetent" (p.14). Participation in multicultural workshops produced such sentiments as being more confident and competent in dealing with those different from oneself.

In discussing the perceptions of women seeking positions in educational administration, Seldin and Calabrese (1987) make points which may be valid for Black applicants as well. They state that the low representation of females in such jobs are related to two specific areas: the frustration and acceptance factors. "The frustration factors is a certain sense of futility attached to applying for top slots" (p. 1). It is felt there is no use to even try. The acceptance factor adheres to an acceptance by minorities that they are not worthy of administration positions. They have bought into the stereotype about abilities and characteristics which seem to preclude them from administration.

The background of this study is affected as well by the concepts of satisfaction and motivation. Black aspirants to administration must believe the job will provide them with a package of satisfactions. There should be a perception that their own particular needs will be met; this, it is noted by such authorities as Maslow (1970), Alderfer (1972), and Herzberg (1966), is diversely influenced via a myriad of environmental, societal, and cultural experiences which may be quite different for the African-American than for his/her white counterparts. Therefore, Blacks may have an entirely diverse set of needs and how these needs might be best satisfied by an administrative position. Sergiovanni (1987) finds that in examining these differences, a convenient and practical means of addressing conditions that are favorable or unfavorable for the production of successful leadership can be demonstrated" (p.23).

PURPOSE OF THE STUDY

The purpose of this study was to determine the African-American managers' perceptions about factors that impact their career development and job opportunities.

SIGNIFICANCE OF THE STUDY

Based on the assumption that African-American individuals perform effectively in administration, the limited number of Blacks in such positions has an effect on the business world, the Black community, and the individual involved. For example, minority students who have never seen African-Americans in leadership positions are not likely to develop aspirations or values that move beyond traditional stereotypes. An important step toward developing a rational approach in maximizing the talents of the African-American administrator must be the recognition of how perceptions of the role—and his/her place in it may impede advancement. Before talents can be utilized, consideration must be given to how these individuals view the "fit" between themselves and administration.

At present, little information is available on how the black administrator, or aspirants to such positions, view the leadership milieu. Does the black individual feel the rapidly changing workplace coincides with his/her unique experiences, strengths, and cultural baggage? Can even a top position meet needs and bring satisfactions related to black perspectives on achievement, self development and growth, and meaningfulness of the job? Are these and similar elements the same for whites and blacks, or do subtle differences have anything to do with the slow advancement of African-American administrators? The significance of the proposed study rested in the expected gathering of some data concerning the perceptions of Black administrators about the business environment and their view of their own place in it.

RESEARCH QUESTIONS

The following questions guided this study:
1. How do the perceptions of managers of different types of organizations (industry, commerce, services) compare in relation to the African-American managers' qualifications, experience, networking, job opportunities, requirements, discriminatory practices, and promotion or hindrance of career development?
2. How do the perceptions of managers of organizations with affirmative action and incentive programs compare with the perceptions of those managers of organizations without those programs?
3. What are the overall perceptions of respondents regarding African-American managers' career development and opportunities?

4. What is the overall evaluation of respondents regarding African-American managers' level of satisfaction, productivity and job equality, managerial style, and managerial skills?
5. What are the organization' projections regarding African-American managerial positions?
6. What factors affect the access of African-American managers to top managerial positions in the future?

ASSUMPTIONS OF THE STUDY

This study was predicated on the following assumption:

1. African-American administrators and those aspiring to such roles have the needed skills, talents, capabilities, and drive to achieve as their white counterparts.
2. The fact that African-Americans advance more slowly up the career ladder is in part due to remaining traces of racial prejudice and stereotyping by administrators who have certain perception about blacks. However, blacks also have perception, brought about by experiences, culture, history, and so forth, that may play a role in slow advancement as well.
3. These perceptions by African-Americans; once discerned and examined, may then be addressed by those individuals and groups, for example, the African-American Business Managers (AAM), in order to ensure that prospective leadership positions will be filled in larger numbers by black aspirants.

LIMITATIONS OF THE STUDY

This study was concerned solely with the perceptions of black administrators and aspiring leaders about those factors in the business environment, which may account for their slow advancement. Further, those perceptions do not revolve around the undoubted presence of racial bias in the workplace, an element of many studies, but rather focus on how blacks look at the alterations in the leadership role in the information era and what they see as their own role in it. Thus, to be examined are feelings about preparedness, satisfactions and dissatisfactions, needs and how well they might be met, and so forth. These views may, or may not, be similar to those held by other groups. The sampling was, limited to Illinois African-American business managers as recognized in the Walton Survey. Other groups and individuals may hold very different views and perceptions about black advancement, or the responses may be quite alike. Since the study was limited to those AAM members in the State of Illinois who choose to complete and return the questionnaire which was developed, the results cannot be generalized to other states in the country. Also, the perceptions of the respondents varied according to the values, beliefs, experiences, and expectations. The descriptive nature of this study was limited to how accurately the AAM members described their perceptions and how they believed these perceptions may, or may not impede their advancement.

DEFINITION OF TERMS

The following terms were defined according to their use in this study.

- Achievement - successfully completing, through effort, skills and perseverance, an important task, purpose, or goal.

4

- Dissatisfiers - those factors, primarily extrinsic in nature, bound up in the total environment in which a job is performed and that contradict high performance and a meaningful relationship between man and job.
- Needs - physiological and psychological conditions in the environment that people must have in order to survive and develop successfully and that differ across populations and individuals.
- Perceptions - preconceived ideas that form over time through formal and informal social processes, culture, and education and may affect human behavior.
- Recognition - feeling valued, that one's ideas are respected, praise for special effort or accomplishment.
- Responsibility - the freedom to exercise decision making, effect changes, and use judgment in the job role.
- Satisfiers - those factors, primarily intrinsic in nature, that motivate humans to perform at high levels.

Chapter
2
Review Literature

INTRODUCTION

In this chapter, the literature that provides relevancy to the perceptions of black business managers in the workplace, their peers and those both above and below them on the career ladder, and their views of how the information era will affect the advancement of African-Americans to top positions are examined. The literature is reviewed in terms of the relationship between perceptions and advancement and the factors of the work environment as they reflect the particular needs and satisfactions/dissatisfactions of African-American administrators and those who aspire to such positions.

THE HISTORICAL BACKGROUND OF PERCEPTIONS

Several classic social theorists have discussed the role of perceptions in human development and behavior. Mead (1964) suggests that people do not respond directly and instinctively to events themselves, but respond in terms of their interpretation of events. Behavior is guided by their mental images of the world. These may or may not be realistic or factual, still they provide a way in which individuals orient themselves to their world.

Combs and Snygg (1969), in their studies of the perceptual field, find that a positive view of self is learned by the ways in which the individual is treated by others. The "self-actualized" person can identify with others without reference to race, creed, or personality. Such a person is open to experience, hence making change and adjustment easier. A rich and extensive perceptual field provides an understanding of the events in which one is involved.

In another view of perception, the process of extracting meaningful information from the environment, Piaget (1964) notes that it is not merely a matter of reflecting images like a camera, but involves an enormous variety of individual differences. People see things from their own values, education, and moral standards. Thus, some stimuli are more noticeable to some persons than others. According to Piaget, as the person develops his/her egocentrism of perception becomes less bound to the physical aspects and more dependent on attitudes, values, and cultural meanings with which he/she interprets the perceptual world.

Gibson (1969) contends that perception involves filtering and abstraction; the selectivity and richness of meaning attached to perceptions continue to expand in individual ways. Throughout adulthood, an individual's perceptions reflect more and more uniqueness of his/her own experiences.

The black managers' role is the result of years of transformation through history. The study of their role in top management reveals that some black managers occupied positions of power and authority. These were the "position power". This situation changed during the domination of the top management from early turn of the century to the present. During the era, the top managers had begun to transfer some training to black managers by introducing top management and corporate positions. Both may be considered of high influence for the role of subordination of black managers. The business demands black managers' obedience to the government and owners. The top management commands and makes the decisions, while the black managers' role is to obey and be subordinate to top management. The goal is to get black managers involved in upper management so that some would advance into top management. The process starts early, receiving reinforcement through cooperative training, economic development, and government programs to assist in sustaining their businesses.

Early in the black managers' development, they receive different treatment. Top managers received special business training, government support, and the finance from various financial institutions under the condition of certain behavior from black managers. In many situations, the business training would reinforce dependent behavior in black manager for the expected role. Top managers are allowed more business management training, while black managers are induced to be secondary-level business management and participate in passive jobs. Top managers work with other top managers, and blacks work with top managers and black management.

Black managers' perceptions have been building through the years and have a strong influence from their African-American heritage. However, the American culture also permeated the African-Americans after the political changes that occurred in the 1960s and 1970s.

Organized black managers' movements started throughout the twentieth century in America. It was closely tied to social, political, and economic changes of the last century. The industrialization process helped the black managers. Since black managers had been receiving strong cultural and economic influence from the government's programs, black managers received the impact of these ideas and movements.

With the introduction of government support training programs to corporations, the black managers' traditional labor economy was converted into a full-scale capitalistic service system. Economic changes transformed black managers into an income generator. Thousands of black managers entered into these industries that took advantage of traditional top managers' skills. The new economic system led to growing proletarianization and the, appearance of organized labor force movements. The demand for more managers led to the use of Black managers in the work force. Black managers were necessary to handle the increase in corporate and government programs. They were incorporated into the production process, receiving a salary for their management services in the industry and participating in labor problems existing at that time. Their role in the socioeconomic activity of government and corporation managers changed. They were highly discriminated against by being paid lower salaries, having no privileges, and not participation in directives or political life. Black managers were no satisfied with their working conditions and became part of the labor movement.

The struggle for black managers' rights during the sixty decades of this century were a combination of the Civil Rights Movement and the efforts of women business owners. Black managers became aware of the importance of affirmative action laws in order to improve their working conditions. Even though they were relegated to sub-level management types of task, inhibited from education and condemned as inferior managers, they obtained entrance into the working world in considerably inferior conditions. Working conditions were not adequate in the corporations and workshops, considered by labor writers of the epoch as antrum of exploitation and abuse (Boyd & Lawson, 1990). Their salaries were considerably lower, most of the time approximately half of what the top managers were paid.

8

Black managers are still receiving a fraction of top managers' salaries for equal jobs. The income median for a black manager has been a fraction of the top managers throughout history (Black Enterprise 1994). During the 1960s, it was 42.8%; for the 1970s, 60.4%; and for the 1980s, 65.1%. Even though Black managers constitute 39.4% of the work force, the salary received is only a fraction of what a top manager receives for the same job. Salaries and opportunities seem to be different for black managers.

Black managers' participation in the Civil Rights Movement has been recognized since the sixty decades of this century. Their collective efforts induced legislators to present more anti-discrimination laws for blacks' suffrage. After intense battles, this right was approved in 1968. Political right and the development of a new government policy during the 1960s generated dramatic new job opportunities in government and corporations. The situation of Black managers changed considerably. Collective efforts improved their working conditions. The government legislated laws to protect or provide rights equal to top managers. Blacks now have the right to vote, to own businesses, and participate in all activities previously dominated by top managers. The number of black managers that are participating in corporation and government jobs is increasing every year.

Improvement in the managerial level of black managers provides advancement in salary scales, but reality shows that equality has not yet been obtained. Notwithstanding, the scene is changing.

PERCEPTIONS

Perceptions are preconceived ideas that have been formed over time through formal and informal social processes, culture, and education and may affect human behavior in the decision-making process. The way people may perceive things varies among different individuals. People's perceptions are determined by their needs. They receive the influence of attitudes, expectations, motives, interests, and positive and negative past experiences which psychologically may lead to specific behavior (Robbins, 1991).

Certain perceptions may be transformed into negative prejudice that will be attached to the object of prejudice (the individual against whom there is a prejudgement), resulting in a new apparent image different from reality (Metzer, 1979). Individuals may modify or distort the impressions they receive, according to the person's self-concept; it is perceived depending on what the individual needs or expects to perceive. Sociological and historical frameworks contributed to the modification of managers' perceptions.

African-American managers' perceptions are affected by the American sociological and cultural framework. The black managers have received a strong working heritage with an equal business influence. The top managers have recognized the black manager's role as secondary level-type managing and put specifically with emphasis on Black subordination to top managers. These ideas received the influence of socioeconomic changes and strong influences from the top manager culture.

African-American managers are entering the work force and are upgrading their educational achievement. Nevertheless, blacks are not easily accepted in the work force. Although blacks have greatly improved their educational levels, there is a slow acceptance in top managerial positions. It seems that there is a predetermined set of ideas concerning blacks and their role in society. Race, not values or capabilities, may be influencing the selection of an individual for a position. Perceptions built over the years may be the explanation for this phenomenon.

Researchers have been studying whether or not educated and experienced Black managers can be tapped into for top management. Managerial jobs are few in number and are the most prestigious and highly paid jobs in government and corporations. Traditionally, top managers have occupied these advantageous spots. The controversy is focused on whether Black managers possess the behavioral and psychological attributes necessary to execute managerial positions. The debate is if black managers are sufficiently aggressive, firm, intelligent, competitive, dominant and energetic to move to upper management.

Researchers have found various recurrent perceptions regarding black managers' capabilities for executing managerial responsibilities. These perceptions are: (1) black managers want to do the work and could do well if the system allowed it; (2) black managers can do the work, but do not want to try; (3) black managers are not prepared to do the work and do want to attempt it: (4) prior socialization impedes black managers to handle work, even though they want to do it; (5) lack of technical and administrative skills impede black managers to work, even though they want to: and (6) Black managers want to do the work and could if   theyknew how to gain access to information channels of influence and information, mentors, and others (Palmer, 1990).

Universal perception placing black managers in a subordinate type management work force is responsible for stereotypes or myths about black managers that endured and have filtered their way into corporate minds and offices around the world. This is a stereotypical, generalized characteristic about a group of people. Black managers have been stereotyped for many years, affecting the perception of how they perform in management. Perceptions of individuals with positions of influence may explain black managers' acceptance or non-acceptance in government or corporate management positions. Management is still considered by many as a top manager's world. The corporate management does not allow Black managers to be seriously considered for the ranks of upper management (Naisbitt & Aburden, 1990).

Black managers entered the work force induced by socioeconomic reasons. They needed to work to enrich their business budget and have tried to obtain equality. The struggle to achieve equality is recent. The most important achievements in the history of Black managers in America corresponds to this century.

Obiakor (1991) stipulates that in today's classrooms, African-American students are being mis-educated. Many students are "marginal", at risk of failure, and disconnected from the educational process. Belief in themselves and their ability to compete and taste success is minimal. Sinclair and Ghory (1987) find that because the curriculum, instruction, and school organization does not address the values, culture, and history of Black students, children perceive the concept of education is not for them and has little to do with day-to-day needs of survival. Glasser (1965) believes Black students do not envision themselves as valuable, competent, or responsible human beings. This view detracts from feelings of self-worth and carry over into adulthood with ramifications for success in the work place. Honeman (1990) states that the Black child is left with an elitist, Eurocentric education which alienates and represses him/her, stifling the desire to learn and create. Beane (1990) brings out more than just knowing or not knowing is involved, for real accomplishment "draws on such skills as valuing, problem-solving, reflective thinking, critical ethics, and social action skills" (p.3). Denied the opportunity to hone these components, the black students are hampered not only in attaining perceptual experiences, but also in later advancement possibilities. Gilliland (1988) believes education in America is predicated on a particular values system which is not that of the African American. Those values include "individualism, competition, aggressiveness, subjugation of the environment, and future's orientation" (p.107).

It is suggested that black children be educated in a manner more in keeping with their culture and its unique aspects. However, those values taught in the traditional curriculum are, in effect, those required for the successful individual to advance in mainstream society. Slavin et al. (1990) briefly touch on this issue by finding that while some students have values and needs at odds with the mainstream curriculum and instructional methodology, it is possible to bolster self-esteem, social skills, and feelings of competency without resorting to an Afro-eccentric program which may limit the child for later competition in the workplace.

NINETEENTH CENTURY: TRADE

The maintenance of high rhythms of economic growth among periods of time had been required for the creation of a great amount of social capital. It was significant that AAM, working in union with Illinois politics, advanced and contributed to the service industry's expansions—and consequently to the creation of new AAM networking and the development of new competitive service functions. Particularly visible were the expansion and improvement of services industry facilities during the nineteenth century. During the nineteenth century, the number of AAM in Illinois had increased substantially (Illinois Central Management Service Agency Directory, 1992). Although AAM have made important progress in the past years, they are still socially disadvantaged. Top managers in the state of Illinois still continue to hold privileged positions. This inequality has been considered a reflection of innate differences between the top manager and AAM that provide potential for domination of subordination of AAM, but it is actually a creation of society itself (Macionis, 1991). Societies establish cultural learned differences between top managers and AAM, including how people envision themselves, and how they interact with other individuals, according to Macionis (1991)

Superior management is concerned not only with differences, but how society views top managers and AAM. There is a disparity of power that distinguishes these two categories of humanity.

The traditional superiority given to top managers throughout history can be attached to their strength in numbers. During early history, survival was closely linked to strength and ability of the top manager to satisfy the need of the organization. AAM were at a disadvantage and depend on the protection of government for their subsistence as well as their primary needs to secure work in the service industries with top managers. AAM were at a disadvantage and depended on the protection of government for their subsistence as well as their primary need to secure work in the service industries with top managers. Since AAM were considered inferior, it was their duty to serve and assist top managers. Culture patterns were developed to maintain some degree of superiority over AAM in a firm business organization.

Toffler (1990) describes a change in powers through history. He calls it "powershift". According to Toffler, different historical stages have been identified by different"powers". The Industrial Revolution is represented by power of forces. The Industrial Revolution is denoted by wealth or money, and the present era is represented by knowledge and mind. The future top managers will master knowledge, and "knowledge itself; therefore, they turn out to be not only the source of the highest-quality power, but also the most important ingredient of force and wealth" (Toffler, 1990). Since power was necessary during the Industrial Revolution, top managers dominated this historical stage. The Industrial Revolution gave way for a small number of AAM to enter the work force.

The third and actual stage requires knowledge. Knowledge may be possessed by all and "is the key weapon in power struggles that accompany the emergence of the super-symbolic economy" (Toffler, 1990). Power is derived from knowledge, not from position, as it was before. Toffler states that knowledge will be the central resource of the advanced economy because it reduces the need for labor, time, space, and capital. Individuals need to control knowledge.

The question is, who will control knowledge? Knowledge is obtained using individual intelligence. Researchers indicate that overall intelligence among top managers and AAM do not differ significantly. Since the present era is driven by knowledge, and knowledge can be obtained by both top managers, now AAM may have the opportunity to achieve equality.

The process for AAM advancement to managerial levels has not kept pace with their upgraded educational achievements. One of the main reasons AAM advancement has been restricted is due to the perceptions of top managers.

THE CHANGING ENVIRONMENT

The last decade has shown significant trends in career development for improvement in positions for blacks and minorities. The environment is changing due to government legislation, demographic changes, the growing black managers work force, education, perception changes, and the emerging role of blacks as leaders and managers. Until the late 1960s, illegal discrimination kept blacks, minorities, the aged, and the handicapped in jobs with lower pay and status. Blacks were experiencing negative discrimination or the action directed either against something or someone" (Kossen, 1991). Government interaction was necessary to alleviate injustices.

GOVERNMENT LEGISLATION

After the 1960s, intense government action and laws protected these classes. Since black managers were discriminated against so much by many government and private agencies, all federal laws were applicable. Equal Employment Opportunity (EEO) and Affirmative Action Programs (AAP) are representative legislation that government has taken to protect these groups. EEO prohibits discrimination against any person because of race, color, religion, sex, or national origin. Equal Employment Opportunity includes laws that regulate over all staffing functions. They apply to hiring, firing, compensation, rewarding employees, assigning the use of facilities, as well as training and retraining. Affirmative Action (AA) requires the employers actively seek out blacks and other minorities and provide better opportunities and positions. Affirmative Action Programs (AAP) must take aggressive steps in trying to recruit and promote blacks, minorities, handicapped, and veterans. They must monitor the percentages of these protected classes in the local labor force. Goals and timetables for recruiting blacks, minorities, the handicapped, and veterans are also set. In this country, some companies enforce Affirmative Action up to the point that they reward their managers financially for meeting "Affirmative Action" targets. In America, this incentive is still unknown. The government legislated to stop discriminatory and prejudiced actions but, as per Garland (1991), in her article presented in Business Week:

> Labor's 18-month study of promotion practices found that entrenched attitudes prevent
> minorities from moving up the corporate ladder-sometimes, not far above entry level. Labor

announced a nationwide crackdown on federal contractors who violate affirmative action laws, although it has the personnel to conduct only limited probes.

According to Garland (1992), corporate eagerness to hire minorities does not guarantee them equal opportunity. Garland states that frustration with career progress, not the managerial abilities and leadership is responsible for most departures by minority professionals. She quotes research by Wick & Company, a Wilmington, Delaware, consulting firm, that indicates that while a large percent of minorities quit large companies and move to other companies, only small percentages stay with the original company. Government legislation is "helping blacks to achieve higher positions, but slowly. Demographics are helping more.

Demographic changes leave companies choices; they have to diversify and start using black managers. Garland (1991) states that "skilled top male comprise a shrinking percentage of the labor—and the customer base". More and more companies are recognizing the need for better utilization of black managers, not only because of their value, but because skilled top managers are losing ground.

The above studies were done across America. They reflect the black managers' situation, since minorities receive a strong socioeconomic influence from the government and a large African-American work force.

MANAGERIAL STYLES

Billard (1992) presents a controversial issue that is actually debated by executives, academics, and the media: do AAM have a different management style than their top manager counterparts; and if so, do the consensus-building, participatory methods that are largely attributed to AAM work better than the hierarchical, quasi-militaristic model. According to Rosener, as quoted by Billard (1992), AAM are more likely than top males to manage in an interactive style, sharing power and information, enhancing the self-worth of individuals and inspiring participation. Rosener established differences when AAM claimed "that AAM tend to use 'transformational' leadership, motivating others by transforming their self-interest into the goals of the organization, while top managers use 'transactional' leadership, doling out rewards for good work and punishments for bad". Billard presents the issue that these theories have defenders and attackers. The defenders argue that AAM strengths would be tapped, even celebrated, while the critics argue that any stereotyping by gender is a form of sexism, one that will only confine women to their traditional role as nurturers. Defenders think minorities and female style of leadership is a better alternative for difficult times.

> In an era when the need to motivate is so important, minorities, and women will do better because they are nurturers and value-driven and at a time when the corporation needs restructuring. AAM will be able to do so because they operate in webs rather than pyramid-shaped hierarchies.

Other defenders believe the styles of AAM are more consistent with the kind of organizations that will be competitive in coming years. Even when many are attaching a distinctive management style for AAM, the same style has been used by some top managers since the early 1980s. Jack Welch from General Electric has been practicing this as a strategy to raise productivity since the early 1980s, which is necessary for staying competitive in the 1990s. According to Billard, he is not alone; and there are plenty of top managers who use "transformational management". Thus, it is not a matter of race. It is a global competition that is changing rules and norms of business. The AAM and top managers exploring and defining

13

transformational leadership are offering a vital and increasing successful option for change (Billard, 1992).

Research evidence favors the position of no gender differences in management (Power, 1990). According to this research, managers of different gender do not seem to differ in any significant way in performing their tasks. AAM managers tend to be more people-oriented than top managers, nor do they tackle task-oriented jobs less effectively than top managers. There were no differences in motivational tests, but "AAM managers were more concerned with opportunities, growth, autonomy, and challenge" and presented a "more and higher-achieving motivational profile" than their top manager counterpart. Subordinate reaction varies; but once subordinates have worked for both AAM and top managers, the effect of stereotypes disappear and managers are treated as individuals rather than representatives of AAM (Power, 1990). The doors of management are opening slowly for AAM because they are demonstrating that AAM and top management are equally capable of inspiring commitment and bringing out the best in people" (Naisbitt & Aburdene, 1990).

As an opinion, AAM may wish to follow the top managers' model of management and power. But, according to Dow (1990), AAM is not following the model of leadership. They are leading by charisma, not fear, sharing power and sharing decision making. They motivate their staff by building self-respect, not by intimidation. In their working relations AAM are softening the rigidly impersonal and competitive relationships between AAM and top managers. They are incorporating more humanity into their leadership style, and are earning power slowly with their unique style.

According to Naisbitt and Aburdene (1990), it is no longer valid to command through authority. Business leadership must win loyalty, achieve commitment, and earn respect. They argue that the new work force cannot be ordered, it responds to democratic leadership and financial incentives, and recognizes that people also belong to another institution—the family. Managing the new work force is a challenge because mental tasks have replaced mechanical ones, and it is almost impossible to "supervise" information work.

AFRICAN-AMERICAN MANAGERS: LEADERS AND MANAGERS

Research has demonstrated that myth and supported opinions that classify blacks as undeveloped individuals must be eradicated. The need to recognize that there are no significant differences between the capabilities of top managers and AAM to perform a job is obligatory. There are some minor differences but no "consistent differences in problem-solving ability, analytical skills, competitive drive, motivation, leadership, sociability, or learning ability" (Power, quoted by Robbins, 1991). In the minor differences found, psychological studies establish that "African-American Managers are more willing to conform to authority and that top managers are more aggressive and more likely than blacks to have expectations of success..." (Maccoby, quoted by Robbins, 1991). But there is no basis to assume that job productivity is lower in black managers than in top managers. In management, "Top managers and black managers are equally capable of inspiring commitment and bringing out the best in people (Naisbitt & Aburdene, 1990).

An increasing number of organizations are aware of the great potential Black managers offer. These organizations are making genuine efforts to attract skilled Black managers and provide opportunities for promotion and development. Consequently, the work force shows an increasing proposition of Black managers, and their number in managerial positions is growing.

Many African-American managers have difficulty in being promoted beyond middle-management jobs. Some critics argue that blacks have lost ground in the past decade and call for renewal of activist tactics. They argue that at the current rate, it will be centuries before blacks reach equality in executive suites. It seems to be impossible to break through the "glass ceiling" the invisible barrier that impedes blacks' access to top managerial positions, in a credible and advantageous time frame. The sense of inequality is universal in top AAM executive positions who perceive their rate of progress as slow and their pay disadvantage in comparison to top manager executive positions. The number of qualified blacks will soon be so great that ignoring them will not be discriminatory, but a bad business decision. According to Holt (1990), there is still discrimination; and in many instances blacks are fighting, even though many companies are actively trying to promote capable Blacks and their role in the work force.

According to Naisbitt and Aburdene (1990), in their book <u>Megatrends 2000</u>, the number of working minorities has increased since World War II, and in the last two decades minorities have obtained two-thirds of the millions of new jobs created in the Information ERA. Blacks are showing some specific characteristics. Whenever they are not restricted by job advancement and opportunities, they are likely to work harder than top managers.

Black aggressiveness was demonstrated when they slightly increased their work force percentage from a minority in 1970 in areas such as banking, accounting, and computer science. This change is even more dramatic if the time frame evaluated is lengthier. According to Vago (1989), there is a dramatic increase in the number of working minorities in the labor force since 1900; from about 5 million then to over 50 million today. He concludes that there are several factors contributing to the current high level of labor force participation among blacks. Among the reasons presented, he mentions: rising education attainment of blacks; economic growth during the 1960s, the Civil Rights Movement, changes in attitudes about desirability (and necessity) of working and rising consumption aspirations of AAM as consumers. The same reasons are affecting other minorities, including the women's work force. The economic growth during the 1970s experienced in America increased AAM participation in the work force. The rising education attainment of AAM is evidenced by statistics presented in 1900 by the United States Department of Labor.

It has been widely accepted that managers are leaders who get things done through other people. Basically, managers are needed in all aspects of lives. All types of organizations need management at all levels. Managers are individuals that execute the functions of planning, organizing, staffing, leading, and controlling to obtain goals or objectives. There are significant characteristics and skills that are expected in these "special individuals". Managers are expected to be intelligent, educated, and have broad analytical interests and capabilities. They are expected to have the ability to manage their own personal affairs successfully and demonstrate excellent personality traits, especially the ability to relate to people. Managers' skills of competencies help them to successfully achieve their goals.

There are three essential management skills: technical, human, and conceptual (Robbins, 1991). It is through technical skills that managers apply specialized knowledge or expertise. Competencies can be learned at school or through formal training or can be developed on the job. In this changing world, managers are aware that they need to update their technical skills continuously; otherwise, the possibility of becoming obsolete or not being able to compete with modern managers may put them out of business.

Other essential requirements are human skills. This is "the ability to work with, understand, and motivate other people, both individually and in groups" (Robbins, 1991). These skills are fundamental to managers since they need to communicate, motivate, and delegate to subordinates in order to accomplish goals. The manager needs other people to get things done, and human skills are the bridge that allow for manager and subordinate interaction. The third essential management skill identified by (Robbins, 1991) is conceptual skill. This is "the mental ability to analyze and diagnose complex situations" (Robbins, 1991). A person may have the technical skills and human skills and still fail because he/she has not mastered conceptual skills.

These three skills are interrelated, but particular emphasis is given to interpersonal roles, or human skills. It has been researched that, "regardless of a manager's level in the organization, human skills are rated most important for his or her success" (Robbins, 1991). It has not been demonstrated that these characteristics are exclusively top manager-oriented.

It is in the 1900s, the last decade of the century and the millennium, that the business community is challenging, changing management styles with "new leadership that will revitalize business and inspire global competitors such as Japanese management did in the 1970s. To a great extent that leadership will come from minorities and women" (Naisbitt & Aburdene, 1990) to be competitive in the global economy.

AAM are starting new businesses twice as fast as other top managers and as "workers, professionals, and entrepreneurs dominate the information society" (Naisbitt & Aburdene, 1990). According to the June 1995 edition of Black Entrepreneur AAM participation is so evident that it is changing prior concepts in identifying workers as top managers. "If the top manager was the prototypical industrial worker, the information worker is typically minority" (Naisbitt & Aburdene, 1990). AAM struggle to breach the invisible boundary or "glass ceiling" that keeps them from the pinnacle. They are exposing themselves as business leaders and demonstrating that they can function as well as their top manager counterparts. If the future requires leaders, AAM are ready to hold fast for these positions.

All dramatic changes and growth are considered by many observers and researchers as a normal path toward an equitable stage in which AAM and top managers may be considered equal. Traditional management concepts are changing. Instead of control, leadership is emerging as the "magic tool" that will assist managers in coping with the global economy. "The dominant principle of organization has shifted from management in order to control an enterprise to leadership in order to bring out the best in people and respond quickly to change" (Naisbitt & Aburdene, 1990). According to Naisbitt and Aburdene (1990), management and leadership are not the same. Not all managers are leaders. Some managers may be short-term, control-oriented, and report oriented. Leaders move their people toward their objectives or goals through "non coercive means" and emphasize respectful relationships, self-management, autonomous teams, and entrepreneur units. They feel this movement causes change. "Leaders recognize that while capital and technology are important resources, people make or break a company" (Naisbitt & Aburdene, 1990).

AFRICAN-AMERICAN BUSINESS MANAGERS

Most of the futurologists agree on the point that AAM will play a very important role in the future. Naisbitt and Aburdene (1990), in their book, Megatrends 2000, consider the AAM role as the new leadership that will revitalize business and inspire global competitors. In their opinion, AAM may have missed out on the industrial age, but they occupy a prominent role in the industries of the future.

In America, "AAM hold a small percent of the executive, administrative, and management jobs" (Bureau of Labor Statistics, quoted by Naisbitt & Aburdene, 1990). The observed trend is growth, and it will continue in the 1900s and into the future. AAM and the information society—which celebrates brain over brawn—are a partnership made... and wherever the information—service sector is AAM, and the work force is well educated, AAM need to be part of the managing group.

The new leader wins commitment by setting an example of excellence: being ethical, open, empowering, and inspiring. AAM are entering the management field without all of the old authoritarian behavior that was considered necessary to manage departments or companies.

During the 1990s and in the future, AAM will have a fertile base to deal with a new tendency in recruiting. Modern leaders are offering flexibility to attract and keep good people. In order to confront expected growing labor shortages during the 1990s, corporations will have to recruit people who did not work in the 1980s. Naisbitt and Aburdene (1990) establish that the source of these undiscovered people will be those who have taken early retirement, disabled people, new immigrants, and non-working AAM caring for their businesses. They consider that the largest potential source are the millions of women and AAM working in their family businesses and that in order to place them in the work force, it will be necessary to establish company-subsidized training programs for executives; flexibility work arrangements in the whole range of professional, technical, manufacturing, part-time, job-sharing, contract work, and family business work arrangements. Flexibility will include benefits and arrangements to provide a good percent of working women and AAM prime training in order to elevate them into top management positions. Management will recognize the need to introduce "planned changes" in these areas in order to take advantage of one resource that will be needed in their industries: women and AAM.

A century ago, there were no women and AAM participating in politics. Women and AAM started voting in the national elections in the United States in the 1920s. Political power of American women and AAM has increased slowly. However, this decade of business leadership is demonstrating women and AAM achieving unprecedented prominence in politics. There are legislators, ministers, governors, mayors, and heads of state with a unique leadership style. The future promises a vast management field for women and AAM. It is up to women and AAM to find these positions, develop skills, and combine them with extensive knowledge of external environments in which business exists, in order to have the ability to be in top management. Future descendants will wonder why the past generations did not offer women and AAM the same opportunities that top managers have had. They will consider it as normal to see either women, AAM, and top managers directing business, government or not-for-profit organizations.

ORGANIZATIONAL STRUCTURE
AND THE NEED OF BLACK ADMINISTRATORS

Maslow (1970), in his classic ideas on human needs, postulates five levels of universal needs: physiological needs, safety needs, social needs, esteem needs, and self actualization needs. A widely known measure of Maslow's theory is one designed by Porter (1975). Porter modified Maslow's hierarchy by eliminating physiological needs on the grounds they are widely satisfied and have little effect on managerial attitudes on work. Instead, he placed the need for autonomy between esteem and self-actualization needs. It is interesting to note that a later study by Anderson and Iwanicki (1984) in the area of education administration, sees significant note for desire for security needs in terms of desire for salary increases, benefits, and job security. They hold that in a tightening labor market and reductionism staff, safety needs come to the fore, displacing the higher needs. It is possible that among Black managers also, safety needs might be more important than in the case of their white peers. African-Americans on the first rung of the administration ladder may sense they are more vulnerable in an era of downsizing. Further, some Blacks must assist parents and other relatives who have not enjoyed the ability to invest, own homes, and other sources of wealth for the white middle class. This factor, too, might place safety needs before higher needs satisfaction.

Herzberg, Mausner, and Snydertnan (1987), take another route in exploring human need and the workplace. They find a two-factor theory is evident: job satisfiers (motivators) and job dissatisfiers (hygiene factors). Hygiene factors are roughly equivalent to Maslow's lower-level needs because they serve to reduce dissatisfaction without leading to satisfaction. They include salary, context of job, company policies, interpersonal relations, and working conditions. Satisfiers, on the other hand, are associated with the job itself, for example, the work content, recognition, achievement, responsibility, advancement, and growth. Some researchers, such as Lunenburg and Ornstein (1991), question whether or not the two dimensions are mutually exclusive and perceive ample proof of overlap in need fulfillment from both the satisfiers and supposed dissatisfiers. Much of what Biklin and Brannigan (1980), discern about women in administration may well have relevance to blacks as well. They find that minorities face dissatisfiers associated with competence and talent when they strive for success in a field dominated by (white) men. To cope, they must confront the psychological stress of internal ambivalence. They examine their career goals to determine their level of aspirations and develop strategies to handle traditional career pressures and struggles with cultural norms and values. Motivational difficulties for minorities in administration are due to a need to prove their competency continuously. In much the same vein, Gordon (1983, notes that in a world with few role models, minorities take on the traits they find around them, whether or not these fit their own needs and satisfactions- dominance, aggression, and striving to achieve. In a workplace dominated by white males, they feel they must be better than their counterparts in the same or similar positions. Therefore, they may well intensify white male managerial patterns and become overly dominant and aggressive. Yet in the selection of minorities for top-level jobs, self-motivation and the determination are the two needs deemed most significant.

ADMINISTRATIVE "CULTURE"
AND THE AFRICAN-AMERICAN MANAGER

In an older book, Arguers (1964), a recognized authority in the management field, writes of "integrating the individual into the organization culture". It is taken for granted this must occur for the good of both the organization and the individual. Yet, not all African Americans have the same goals when they enter the administrative culture. Some do wish to assimilate completely into the standards, values, and morals of the environment, but others prefer to keep their own cultural features, whether or not these are in keeping with the new setting. The question is if this is possible in the climate of the workplace. Interestingly, Toffler (1990), asserts that in the information era, culture "is growing more, not less important" (p.340). Rather than a homogenizing of the workplace and elsewhere, as it took place in the "second wave", diversity is occurring as "all strain to retain or enhance their cultural individuality". Thus diversity would be expected and accepted in the organization, and, indeed, welcomed. But is this the actual reality? Heilman and Hornstein (1982), predicate organizational culture on several propositions: that organizations are created and exist for the purpose of achieving certain goals; that the organization's structure and process are determined by those goals; that behavior in organizations is governed by the norms of rationality; and the goals, tasks, technologies, and structures are the primary determinants of organizational behavior—the needs, emotions, self-interests, values, and attributes of individuals or groups are less significant. These are best assimilated into the "melting pot" of the organization's processes. Only in this way can communications be imported, trust and cooperation fostered, and participation in securing goals be insured. Yet, as pointed out by Bohlman and Deal (1985), "organizations exist ultimately to serve human needs rather than vice versa". Because organizations are critically dependent on their abilities to make effective use of human energies and talents, humans, in all their diversity, can have a critical impact on the organizational culture; thus, organizational culture does not merely have impact on the person. However, when human and organizational cultures collide, when needs differ, those voices should be heard. But if those needs disrupt the mission of the organizational culture, boundary relations have to be so managed as to bring the two into rough balance" (p.202).

Several writers, most notably Robbins (1991) and Lewis (1985), discuss the new organizational culture in which managerial style more nearly accommodates differing needs and values. In certain instances, this may increase the potential of the black administrator, who may be more inclined toward a participatory, facilitating, nurturing type of leadership. These attributes not only match his/her needs, but are more in tune with today's cultural direction.

ORGANIZATIONAL DIRECTORS
AND BLACK ADMINISTRATIVE OUTLOOK

Writers such as Jones et al. (1988) and Drucker (1982), have traced the purposes, environmental forces, human interactions, and hierarchical structures that have communality to organizations. The "healthy" organization moving in a positive directions is one that can continuously maintain itself in its environment. It is constantly developing and engaging in coping activities so that it can extend its utility. Among its dimensions is the ability to foster in its workers: innovation, creativity, and a degree of autonomy. Long dominated by the "Theory X" philosophy of management, one that embraces control and authority, the new direction is more supportive of "Theory Y". This view supplies higher order need fulfillment and allows for more self-control, self-direction, and autonomy. As the African-American business manager looks at the organization, what are his/her perceptions of management looks at the organization, what are his/her perceptions of management style?

The black manager may see in Theory X, an approach which favors strong, dynamic leadership with its stress on responsibility for outcome resting with the administrator. Hersey et al. (1988), looks at this management style in depth. Those who select such a structure are deemed over controlling, excessively competitive, uncomfortable with feelings, and closed to ideas other than their own. Democratic, participative concepts were looked upon as "unworkable". It is highly likely that most black managers would not choose, consciously at least, this theory for action. It is possible, however, that subconsciously, African-Americans might view this organizational behavior as demonstrating their ability to "get things done", to take responsibility, and to show competency and ability to "take charge". Yet more in accord with what is held "Black learning styles" and socialization experiences, as noted by Asante (1987) and McClelland (1988), in motivation, are the "softer" management styles. Kinship and peer groups, for example, play a major role in the socialization of black children, rather than external sources such as television and schools in mainstream society. Hence, it may be found that Black managers are highly sensitive to group dynamics and the role it plays in the organization. Regarding, employees as passive, dependent, and in need of tight control could be discerned as "cutting too close to the bone" as it relates to stereotyping in respect to blacks as a population.

This study focuses on a problem that has not been investigated before in the State of Illinois. Differences between top managers and African-American Managers (AAM) have been discussed for years. Top managerial superiority is always argued. Management styles of top managers and AAM do not provide absolute evidence for this controversy. Therefore, a rather unusual approach to the literature review has been adopted by this researcher. Indeed, a survey of the literature will indicate that some studies on the perceptions of African-American Managers concerning the economic and labor effects of the politics with the State of Illinois government contracts on the stability of service contracts received by AAM will be conducted, but to date, no study has been investigated. Consequently, theories and concepts which might account for this study are included in the literature review.

As a starting point, a conceptual framework will establish a common meaning for essential concepts and also provide a similar frame of reference for the reader. To illustrate how Illinois politics affects the AAM service industry labor force, the framework portrays relationships among three concepts: unemployment, top managers and AAM, and the service industry. Most important, the framework provides a rational explanation as to how and why the various elements concerned with the study—labor force, perception of top managers of AAM, service industry and Illinois economy are related.

In the next section, a theoretical orientation is analyzed in terms of the conceptual framework. The subsequent deals with the literature concerning the categories of the Illinois AAM service industry labor force, competition, government, and the economy. Career development and job opportunities constitute the main segment. The economic history is substantial in the statement and analysis of how top managers satisfy their wishes and needs. However, it is not precise to fully accept all material premises of history, nor the most extreme conclusions, to understand the crucial function performed by top managers in Illinois' economic development.

The impressive AAM development during recent years, in all aspects, is not conceivable without the huge growth of the top managers in the service industry that made the Industrial

Revolution and the next events possible. Illinois AAM is not an exception of this general phenomena.

The basic postulate is that service industry changes and Illinois' political relations with the top managers are the two real variables of autonomies in Illinois AAM development. Business service in Illinois, in particular its economic dimensions, is being developed for AAM in the historical context, particularly in Illinois. It is important to relate what has occurred through the years with AAM in businesses who tried to work their way up in business.

AAM history can be divided in two great periods—before and after World War II. AAM were isolated by the principle modernization tendency. The economy productivity was inadequate to attain a long-run decisive development, and society lacked the corresponding attributes of the most progressive service industry.

Contemporary Illinois has a service industrialized economy and has acquired, in the process, other economic modernization characteristics. AAM history can be divided in two great ages as mentioned before. The first AAM history years can be subdivided into various periods, each one with its own characteristics. The first would be the years of colonization, 1920 to 1970; fifty years that included World Wars I and II, as well as the Vietnam Conflict that ended in the year 1974. The second was the first five decades of this century. The subsequent years constitute the second great age of AAM history.

During the first 20 of the 50 years Illinois AAM was divided into two areas: Black business managers who ran their companies without the help of the government, and Black business managers whom the government was developing.

The second period is the 40 of the 50 years that started in the 1940s. At the end of this period, the AAM society was established (James Pott, 1903). It was an era dedicated substantially to the development of AAM, service industry and education, and the establishment of separated business.

The third period corresponds to the years between 1950 and 1970. Commercial, political, and economic relations with the government was adopted, and training between top managers and AAM were established. There was an expansion and modernization in the service industries. Illinois commerce and investment was slow to the development of AAM. Economic development took place in Urban Developments. The establishment of government programs made AAM formation in service and management professions possible. New political and economic union with Illinois politics was important for AAM's economic development during those years.

The years beginning in 1980 could be considered as the modern period of AAM history. The predominance of top managers in government carried a series of events that made a great variety of economic activities possible, expanding the AAM program, improving government AAM relations, and principle modernization of the service industry. During these years, social reform programs, economic development, structures rationalization and. modernization, and public administration procedures were formulated.

African-American Managers' Work Force and Competition

In 1963, the Equal Pay Act was approved. Its intention was to forbid discrimination and ensure the same salary for the same kind of work, without considering race. This movement improved working conditions for blacks, but there are still differences in the salaries between top managers and blacks. The United States Bureau of the Census in 1988 shows that in the selected occupational categories of top managers. The Equal Pay Act stopped many abuses, but substantial differences are common today.

The last census shows that even when blacks have improved their situation in managerial positions, there is a long way to go before obtaining equality. The relationship of top managers and black participation in selected managerial positions in state government or private corporations will be illustrated.

In addition to government legislation, education is playing a dramatic role in changing the work environment. Today's work force is well educated. Due to blacks improving their education, they are entering into new jobs in the Information Era. It is part of the changing environment that is providing blacks with a dynamic, increasing work force. During the 1980s, blacks received more degrees conferred by higher education institutions. In 1990, African-American enrollment in educational institutions represented a higher percentage of the college population.

The census of 1990 identifies that from the population of 18 year-olds and over, top managers have a high school diploma or higher education, while more blacks possess a high school or higher education. These statistics will illustrate a more educated black manager population, with blacks 18 years old and over, showing an increase in achieving high school diplomas and/or better academic preparation. Top managers of the same characteristics are at or slightly under the average percentage of blacks. Blacks are entering postgraduate education looking for the springboard to high-prestige jobs. Now they aspire higher education; before it was considered unnecessary because most of the majority were not managers. Unfortunately, the black managers' work force is facing "structural misemployment", or the employment of individuals with higher qualifications than required, causing a mismatch of skills or preparation and requirements of available jobs.

According to Vago (1989), American minorities are postponing marriage, prompted by their desire to complete their education and start careers prior to contracting marital responsibilities. Since they have control over their family life, they can schedule more time to improve their education and careers.

Koretz (1992) in his article, "America's Neglected Weapon: Its Educated Women", in Business Week presents a study by the Education Department researcher, Clifford Adelman, in which minorities are considered a critical, underutilized resource in the economy. The study's emphasis is in the consistently superior academic performance by blacks in high school and college. It did not matter if blacks were in a high or low socioeconomic status; their average class rank is superior. In college, they win scholarships and earn degrees sooner, and their attitude toward education is more positive than top managers. The study also states that the labor market' is not rewarding blacks for good academic performances. According to Adelman, U.S. minorities of all races are the best educated and trained in the world. This is evidenced by the superior performance of more than half of all black enrollees and degree recipients at all levels of higher education except doctoral.

PERSONNEL SELECTION

According to Schmidt, Ones, and Hunter (1992), "much good research in personnel selection appears in unpublished technical reports; e.g., in the case of military and government research, which is sometimes the best supported in terms of resources, sample sizes, and other critical factors" (p. 628)

Overall, validity generalization (VG) generates much research, but the questions studied are becoming more micro and less macro; many articles are examinations of potential fine tunings. The larger questions appear to be in areas of application of meta-analysis outside of personnel selection (Hunter & Schmidt, 1990a). However, this is a positive development, indicating the maturing of what was viewed ten years ago as an abrupt paradigm shift in personnel selection. The big questions in VG today appear to be not in the scientific but in the applications domain. For example, will the Supreme Court's Wards Cove decision mean increased use of VG by employers? What are the implications of the Civil Rights Bill of 1991 and of the U.S. Department of Labor's proposed two-year suspension of the General Aptitude Attitude Battery Test (GATBT)? The answers to these questions will depend on the societal struggle to balance the competing values of economic efficiency and competitiveness, on the one hand, and equality, on the other.

Schmidt et al. (1992) contend that aptitude and ability tests continue to be a major focus of research in personnel selection. Anastasi (1989) as quoted by Schmidt et al. (1992), presents an overview of some major trends in ability and aptitude testing, including the increasing emphasis on theory and construct validation, item response theory, validity generalization, and the responsibilities of test users. An informative book-length integrative review of validity studies conducted on the Armed Services Vocational Aptitude Battery (ASVAB) is now available (Welsh et al., 1990). This is accompanied by an extensive annotated bibliography of ASVAB studies, with abstracts of each study. The importance of these two documents is enhanced by the fact that most of the studies covered are not in the published literature but are available as technical reports to the researcher who knows what to ask for.

An attempt to validate the ASVAB for civilian occupations (Armstrong et al., 1988) was crippled when the Office of Management and Budget (OMB) refused to allow gathering of criterion data; as a result, the criterion used was membership in occupations rather than performance. Hence, Hunter (1986), had previously shown that several of the key constructs in the ASVAB are identical to their counterpart in The General Aptitude Test Battery (GATE), thus making GATE validity evidence relevant. Also, Austin and Hanisch (1990) found in a large-sample longitudinal study using Project Talent data (1990) that mental ability scores obtained by high school sophomores were the best predictors of occupational attainment eleven years later. Research relating the general mental ability component of the ASVAB to hands-on performance measured by job sample tests in the three armed services has found substantial validity that is stable over the four years of the enlistment period (Office of the Assistant Secretary of Defense, Force Management and Personnel, 1990). Although people at all levels of aptitude improved with job experience, differences between higher and lower-aptitude personnel persisted, replicating earlier findings (Schmidt et al., 1988b)

In May 1990, the United States Office of Personnel Management introduced a new nationwide examination for college graduates seeking government careers. For each of six job families, test of verbal and quantitative reasoning abilities have been developed that are cast in terms of concrete tasks appearing on those jobs. The tests are unique in that they are constructed using the principles of Logic Based Measurement (Colberg & Nestor, 1987; Colberg, 1985), which ensure that all relevant facets of deductive and inductive reasoning are covered and that the keyed correct answers are logically correct. The exam also include a biodata component (discussed below). Initial validity findings for the exam have been encouraging.

The use of meta-analysis to calibrate the absolute and relative validities of selection procedures more precisely requires the availability of validity studies. One solution to this problem is the new Test Validity Yearbook edited by Professor Frank Landy of Pennsylvania State University. Some thirty-five manuscripts have been accepted, and Volume I was expected in 1991. Ash et al. (1990) reported a survey of selection methods used by urban and state police. The percentages of forces using the various methods were: cognitive ability, 92%; personality tests, 68%, biodata, 35%; and physical strength and ability, 80%. Based on a sample of almost 300 managers, Schippman and Prien (1989) reported an uncorrected correlation of .35 between general mental ability and rate of managerial progression (age-corrected managerial rank). Most studies relating ability to managerial success have used ratings, making this study an improvement. Campion (1989) reported evidence that designing or redesigning jobs to increase their motivating potential (motivational attributes) may also increase the levels of general mental ability required, and hence could affect selection and compensation practices.

Prediger (1989) challenged the conclusion (Hunter, 1986; Jensen, 1986; Thorndike, 1986) that general ability is more important in determining occupational level and job performance than specific abilities, but he presented no data on validity or incremental validity. His conclusion that specific aptitudes are important in performance was based on data showing distinct patterns of specific aptitude means across occupations, both among incumbents and among high school students who later entered specific occupations. However, validities can be equal for different occupations when means are different. Prediger seems to have overlooked the possibility, predicted by the investment theory of ability, that interests determine both (a) the specific skills (e.g., mechanical) that the individual "invests" his general ability in developing, and (b) job choice. If interests determine both relative standing on specific aptitudes (within the individual) and job choice, this would explain why specific aptitudes contribute little beyond general ability to prediction of job performance.

Despite the cumulative evidence for substantial validity, biodata scale are infrequently used. In a survey of 248 firms, Hammer and Kleiman (1988) found that only 6.8% of firms stated that they had never used biodata in employment decisions, and only 4% indicated they currently use biodata scales. The most frequent reasons for not using it were: lack of knowledge; lack of methodological expertise; and lack of personnel, money, and time. Large minorities of respondents also expressed concerns about Equal Employment Opportunity and invasion of privacy risks. Clearly, human resource managers could benefit from education about biodata.

A key assumption in biodata is that past behaviors–often behaviors far in the past; e.g., high school achievements- are good predictors of future behaviors. However, Kleimman and Faley (1990) found biodata items inquiring about present behaviors were just as valid as those focusing on past behaviors in predicting intention to re-enlist in the Air National Guard. If this finding holds for other criteria, some rethinking of a basic assumption will be required. Russell et al. (1990) found that retrospective life-history essays could serve as the source of valid biodata items, and Russell (1990) found some suggestions that structured interviews could also serve a such a source.

A review of the literature between 1982 and 1989 (Harris, 1989) indicates that interviews can have higher average validities than researchers have traditionally believed, and the validities are generalizable (McDaniel et al., 1990; Wiesner & Cronshaw, 1988). The mean corrected validity across all interview types is .45 (McDaniel et al., 1990); even for unstructured interviews the operational validity is surprisingly high at .40 (McDaniel et al., 1990). wright et al., (1989) meta-analyzed structured interview validities. For employment interviews with job performance criteria, meta-analysis results indicate residual standard deviations smaller than those for ability tests. Despite differences in jobs, constructs measured, and other factors, there appears to be little room for moderators to operate. Studies have lent support to the proposition that there is no evidence of sex discrimination in interviewer evaluations of applicant qualifications (Gardner & Discenza, 1988: Graves & Powell, 1988). Alternative ways of conducting interviews have been studied. Motowidlo et al. (1989), found that a paper and pencil situational inventory for entry-level management positions correlated from .28 to .37 (uncorrected) with job performance ratings. However, the authors acknowledged that the situational inventory was essentially a test of "practical intelligence". Martin and Nagao (1989) compared face to face, paper and pencil, and computerized verions of the interview and found there was less social desirability in responses when impersonal modes of interviewing were used by the applicants. They resented impersonal interviews.

From the legal point of view, Spencer (1989) provides a summary of recent Supreme Court rulings on preferential hiring and reverse discrimination and identifies properties she feels are necessary to make affirmative action plans (AAPs) legally defensible. The tradeoffs for using AAPs are usually viewed as between economic efficiency and social equity. However, the adverse political reactions of non-preferred groups must also be considered. Warner and Steele (1989) report the results of three Gallup Polls in which the public was asked to choose between selection based on "preferential treatment" as a remedy for past discrimination and selection "determined by ability test scores". In all the polls, approximately 10%- chose preferential treatment and more than 80% chose selection based on ability test scores. Sowell (1989) pointed out that the public supports special educational and vocational courses for minority groups, and stated, "The issue is not simply whether one is for or against the advancement of particular groups or is willing to see transfers of resources for their betterment. The method by which their betterment is attempted matters greatly. " Affirmative Action Plans that result in lowering of valid standards in selection are unacceptable to many people.

Schmidt et al. (1992) argued that considerable progress has been made in understanding job-performance ratings. However, much evidence now exists that single-rater reliability above .50 are rarely to be expected, that halo should perhaps not be viewed as error, and that complex rating-scale technologies do not improve job performance ratings. Also, there is increasing evidence that validity of many predictors do not decline with increasing time intervals, although research on this question will (and should) continue. Progress has been made in elucidating the constructs underlying job performance. Finally, there is increasing interest in developing explanatory theories of job performance, stimulated in part by the fact that research has provided stable and precise estimates of the relationship among many variables. Efforts to develop such theories are an indication that the field is maturing (p.661). From a broader perspective, the present period is one of both dramatic progress and clear dangers for personnel solution (p. 662).

CONCLUSIONS

Although little direct literature pertains to how African-Americans perceive the administration of organizations, a small body of information can be applied to the problem. The business community is in an era of rapid change, as Toffler so clearly brings out. Management styles, needs, experiences, and values may well favor the increased pace of advancement for the Black administrator, yet how he/she looks at the management task is as critical as how the management regards those African-Americans seeking that advancement. While views of top managers who still dominate the top slots is important, it is also vital to gain understanding of how the views of blacks play just as vital a part in the advancement process. As the literature shows, blacks with their unique needs, experiences, values structure, and human skills will display these factors in the dawning of the new information era.

Chapter

3

Methodology

The purpose of this study was to determine the African-American managers' perceptions about factors that impact their career development and job opportunities. This chapter includes the design of the study, definition of variables, description of the population and sample, description of the instrument, validation and reliability of the instrument, research procedure, and procedure for statistical analysis.

DESIGN OF THE STUDY

The proposed study was predicated upon descriptive research. In this methodology, there was a systematic analysis and description of the facts and characteristics of African-American managers. The descriptive research used involved the analysis, recording, description, and interpretation of conditions that existed, which according to Best (1981), denote this style of research. It also involved a contrast or comparison and attempts to discover any which were present between perceptions and advancement opportunities. Comparisons were made between perceptions of black managers about their needs, satisfactions/ dissatisfactions and leadership style and those which 70 prevailed in predominantly top lead business organizations.

According to Williamson (1981), the descriptive studies supply the researcher with a detailed accounting of a population, event or situation, and are useful in examining relationships between phenomena. "Descriptive research attempts to describe the existing behavior, opinions, attitudes or other characteristics of the group or culture under study" (Drew, 1980).

Definition of Variables

The relationship between the dependent and independent variables were defined in order to identify the African-American managers' perceptions about factors that impact their career development and job opportunities. The dependent and independent variables were according to the research questions, the following:

DEFINITION OF VARIABLES

1. How do the perceptions of the managers of different types of organizations (industry, commerce, service) compare in relation to the African-American manager' qualifications, experience, networking, job opportunities and requirements?

Dependent	Independent
Qualifications	Types of Organization
Networking	
Requirements	
Job Opportunities	

27

2. How do the perceptions of managers of organizations with affirmative action and incentive programs compare with the perceptions of those managers of organizations without those programs?

Dependent	Independent
Perceptions	Organizations with or
Qualifications	without affirmative
Networking	actions or incentive
Requirements	programs

3. What are the overall perceptions of respondents regarding African-American managers, career development and job opportunities?

Dependent	Independent
Overall perceptions	Types of Organizations
regarding career	
development and job	
opportunities.	

4. What is the overall evaluation of respondents regarding African-American managers level of satisfaction, productivity, and job quality, managerial style, managerial skills?

Dependent	Independent
Overall evaluation	Types of Organizations
regarding satisfaction,	
productivity, equality,	
style, and skills	

5. What are the organizations' projections regarding African-American managers' managerial positions?

Dependent	Independent
Organizations'	Types of Organizations
Projections	

6. What factors affect the access of AfricanAmerican managers to top managerial positions in the future?

Dependent	Independent
Factors that affect	Types of Organizations
access to top	
managerial positions	

DESCRIPTION OF THE POPULATION AND SAMPLE

As previously noted in Chapter I, the universe of the study was African American managers in the State of Illinois. These African-American managers were selected from the 1993 Illinois Central Management Directory. This universe consisted of 600 individuals so listed. From the universe, a sample was drawn. This sampling was composed of 25% of the universe of 600 subjects. The sample size was 150 subjects selected at random.

DESCRIPTION OF THE INSTRUMENT

To measure African-American managers' perceptions, a questionnaire was developed by the researcher. The criteria used were those Bog and Gall (1983) described: (1) attractiveness; (2) ease with which it can be completed; (3) number of items and pages; (4) sequence, coding, and print, and (5) explanation of the relevance of the questionnaire. The response codes were designed with a Likert like scale as follows:

1 – Do not know
2 – Strongly disagree
3 – Do not agree
4 – Fairly agree
5 – Strongly agree

In addition, some questions required a brief written response. The total number of questions were 38 in order to avoid unresponsiveness due to length or complexity. The questions dealt with such areas as: what produces most satisfaction/dissatisfaction in the workplace; how one's life experiences may affect such perceptions as those surrounding achievement, responsibility, salary status, peer and supervisor relationships, as well as views about leadership style and advancement potential.

VALIDATION AND RELIABILITY OF THE INSTRUMENT

As noted by Fowler (1988), any instrument is only as worthy as its validity and reliability permit. The format of the questionnaire was of greatest importance for the study. Care was taken to ensure that each question measured the perceptions it was designed to cover. It is expected that an instrument is reliable; that is, repeatable on different occasions with quite similar results. It must be noted that any questionnaire is dependent on the honest answers of those taking part in the study. In addition, problems may arise from the failure of all those selected to respond to the questionnaire for whatever reason. If the sampling thus becomes too small, it can no longer fulfill its desired goals. However, in this instance, because the prospective respondents were professionals, the researcher expected the answers given would reflect real perceptions and that most of the questionnaires would be returned in prompt and orderly fashion.

For the validation of the instrument to be secured, a group composed of four (4) experts in minority business enterprises in the State of Illinois was consulted. They validated the items of the questionnaire in accord with the research questions.

The questionnaire was checked with experienced evaluators. It was validated with reliability testing in a pilot group of 15 managers. This group consisted of African-American managers with the same characteristics of those of the sample. The same questionnaire that was sent to the sampling was administered to the pilot group. The reliability testing was completed and validated using a standardized item alpha that yielded a coefficient of .90. Recommendations were incorporated to the instrument. The instrument was accompanied with a brief introductory letter which stated the purpose of the study and its importance to African-American Management personnel. A self addressed and stamped envelope was also included. This was the process used to test the questionnaires for reliability and internal consistent as well as content validity.

RESEARCH PROCEDURE

The method selected for this research was a descriptive study utilizing a questionnaire. Before administering the questionnaire, the following steps were followed: (1) validation of the questionnaire by a group of experts in minority business enterprises, and (2) a pilot study to ensure the reliability of the questionnaire.

Upon completion of these steps, the final questionnaire was administered to the sample by mail. Once the data were collected, they were summarized and analyzed statistically in order to interpret the findings and answer the research questions. The responses were coded and then analyzed via a computer program written for the purpose.

Quantitative research depends on the construction of tables through which frequencies and percentages of the cases can be demonstrated. Such tables were devised for this purpose. Once the data were analyzed and interpreted, the conclusions, implications, and recommendations of the study were written.

PROCEDURE FOR STATISTICAL ANALYSIS

The data analysis for this study was developed by an IBM-compatible computer using a statistical analysis program called Stat Packets (Statistical Analysis Package).

The scores identified in the questionnaire for each item were processed and summarized with central management distribution utilizing frequency analysis.

The following is the relation between the research questions, statistical analysis method used, and questionnaire items:

- Research Question No. 1:

  How do the perceptions of the managers of different types of organizations (industry, commerce, service) compare in relation to the African-American managers' qualifications, experience, networking, job opportunities, and requirements?

  Statistical Method:

  Descriptive statistics and cross-tabulation between types of organizations (items #1) and qualifications, experience, networking, job opportunities, and
  requirements (items 6-27).

- Research Question No. 2:

  How do the perceptions of managers of organizations
  with affirmative action and incentive programs compare with the perceptions of those managers of organizations without those programs?

  Statistical Method:

  Descriptive statistics and cross-tabulation between organizations without those programs (item #5) and perceptions on qualifications, networking, requirements, and job opportunities (items 6 27).

- Research Question No. 3:

  What are the overall perceptions of respondents regarding African-American managers' career development and opportunities?

  Statistical Method:

  Descriptive statistics and cross-tabulation between types of organizations (item #1) and respondents' perceptions regarding African American career
  development and opportunities (items 28-31).

- Research Question No. 4:

  What is the overall evaluation of respondents regarding African-American managers' level of satisfaction, productivity and job quality, managerial style, and managerial skills?

  Statistical Method:

  Descriptive statistics and cross tabulation between types of organizations (item No. 1) and African-American managers' level of satisfaction, productivity and job quality, managerial style, and managerial skills (items 32-35)

- Research Question No. 5:

    What are the organizations' projections regarding African-American managerial positions?
    Statistical Method:
    Descriptive statistics and cross-tabulation between types of organizations (item 1) and projections regarding African-American managerial positions
    (items 36-37)

- Research Question No. 6:

    What factors affect the access of African American managers to top managerial positions in the future?
    Statistical Method:
    Descriptive statistics and cross-tabulation between types of organizations (item 1) and factors that promote or hinder the access of African-American managers to top managerial positions in the future (item #38)

Chapter

4

Presentation and Analysis of Data

This study was proposed to explore the AfricanAmerican managers' perceptions about factors that impact their career development and job opportunities. The purpose of this chapter is to present the results and findings of this study as guided by the research questions. The results were based on descriptive statistics and cross tabulations of the main variables as measured by the questionnaire. The quantitative data provided a context of socio-demographic descriptions of the subjects who participated in the study. The presentation of the results was organized in two parts. First, the socio-demographic profile of the subjects in terms of relevant variables such as gender, type of organization, education, position held affirmative action programs and years of working experience were presented. For this, summary statistics were used. Second, a cross tabulation technique, using the Chi-Square statistics was used to address the research questions of the study.

SOCIO DEMOGRAPHIC PROFILE OF THE SAMPLE

Gender

Out of 150 questionnaires mailed, 121 subjects answered which represented 81%. As reported by the 121 participants in the study, 47% were males and 53% were females. It is important to mention that eight observations were missing, and that the final count for the sample was 113 which represented 75%. The previous results did not take into consideration the missing cases.

Table 1: Descriptive Statistics for Gender

Gender	Frequency	Percent (%)
Male	53	47
Female	60	53
Total	113	100

WORKING EXPERIENCE

Thirty-two percent (32%) of the sample had five years or less of working experience; Twenty-two percent (22%) had between six and ten years of working experience; eight percent (8%) had between eleven and fifteen years; fourteen percent (14%) between sixteen and twenty years; and twenty-four (24%) over twenty years. These results showed that half of the sample (50%) had less than ten years of working experience and the other half over eleven years. What follows ± a summary that illustrates the findings.

Table 2: Descriptive Statistics for Years of Experience

Years of Experience	Frequency	Percent (%)
Less than 5	36	32
6 through 10	25	22
11 through 15	9	8
16 through 20	16	14
Over 21	27	24
Total	113	100

LEVEL OF EDUCATION

Data on level of education showed that twenty-one percent (n = 24) had completed only a high school diploma. Thirty-three percent (n = 38) had a bachelor's degree; forty percent (n = 46) had completed a master's degree; and six percent (n = 7) had a doctoral degree. These results indicated that about half of the sample had a bachelor's degree or less and the other half had completed higher degrees. They also showed that over seventy-nine percent of the sample had completed college degrees. The following table summarizes these findings:

Table 3: Summary Statistics for Level of Education

Years of Experience	Frequency	Percent (%)
High School	24	21
Bachelor's Degree	38	33
Master's Degree	46	40
Ph.D.	7	6
Total	115	100

AFFIRMATIVE ACTIONS PROGRAMS

Regarding the Affirmative Action Programs or any similar equal opportunity outreach program for furthering the use of African-Americans in management positions, the results showed that forty-six percent had such programs and fifty-four percent did not have the programs. The following table presents the results for this variable.

Table 4: Summary Statistics for Affirmative Action Programs

Affirmative Action Programs	Frequency	Percent (%)
Yes	52	46
No	62	54
Total	114	100

POSITION

Data analysis on type of position held by the managers from the sample (n = 113) showed the following distribution: thirty-two percent indicated that they held executive positions and also professional positions. Thirty-six percent held support staff positions.

Table 5: Summary Statistics for Position Held

Position	Frequency	Percent (%)
Executive	36	32
Professional	36	32
Support Staff	41	36
Total	113	100

RESEARCH QUESTIONS

As mentioned in the methodology section of this study, (Chapter III), the research questions were analyzed using descriptive statistics and cross tabulations. In this section, the researcher presents the results for each one of the questions that guided this research. A general description of the results are presented followed by the appropriate statistical tests. The presentation of results follows the order of the six research questions listed earlier:

Research Question No 1: The first question focused on the issue about how the perceptions of the managers of different types of organizations (industry, commerce, service) compared in relation to the African-American managers' qualifications, experience, networking, job opportunities, and requirements. This question was analyzed cross tabulating the item in the questionnaire (item 1) referring to types of organizations and the items referring to qualifications.

When asked if their firm's needs required academic qualifications that are present in AAM, the results were varied. The variable qualification was measured by items 6, 7, and 37. This cross tabulation yielded a Chi-Square value of 15.13 which was significant at an alpha level of 0.05. This indicated that different types of organizations had a significant different perception about academic qualifications that were present in AAM. It seemed that the difference lied between the industry and the other two: commerce and service. The managers from industry had a higher amount of disagreement than the other two. Forty-one percent disagreed or strongly disagreed in industry versus thirteen percent in service and commerce with zero percent. The percent of agreement was also different when comparing industry versus commerce and service. The percent of agreement was less in industry (59%) when compared with 100% in commerce and 83% in industry (see Table 6).

Table 6: Cross Tabulation of Type Organization by Perceptions Academic Qualification Required

	Perceptions About AAM's Qualifications					
	Industry		Commerce		Service	
	Count	%	Count	%	Count	%
Not sure	0	0	0	0	3	4
Strongly Disagree	2	12	0	0	2	2
Disagree	5	29	0	0	9	11
Agree	1	6	5	39	16	19
Strongly Agree	9	53	8	61	53	64
Total	17	100	13	100	83	100

Chi-square: 15.13, df = 8, p < 0.05

More analysis of perceptions was measured by item 7 in the questionnaire which asked if AAM were academically prepared but exhibited a lack of other needed attributes to become good managers and cross tabulated by time 5. Analyzing this item by type of organization, it indicated a Chi-Square value of 7.43 which was found to be non-significant (p> 0.05). This result revealed that different types of organizations did not have significantly different perceptions regarding AAM. They were academically prepared; and exhibited a lack of other attributes to become good managers. The distribution of answers indicated that the managers of the three different types of organizations disagreed or strongly disagreed in the same way to this question. About 50% of the sample studied disagreed or strongly disagreed and about the same amount agreed or strongly agreed. This showed that there was no significant difference in their perceptions (see Table 7).

Table 7: Cross Tabulation of Type of Organization by Perception of Academic Preparation Required

| | *Perceptions About AAM's Academic Preparation* | | | | | |
| | Industry | | Commerce | | Service | |
	Count	%	Count	%	Count	%
Not sure	0	0	1	8	4	5
Strongly Disagree	7	41	3	23	22	26
Disagree	2	12	5	38	24	29
Agree	6	35	1	8	20	24
Strongly Agree	2	12	3	23	13	16
Total	17	100	13	100	36	100

Chi-Square: 7.43, df = 2, p > 0.05

Further analysis of perceptions was measured by item 37 which asked the respondents to select among candidates from AAM or WM with the same qualifications. The analysis of this item by types of organizations showed Chi Square value of 0.817 with an alpha of 0.66 (p>O.O5). This result revealed that different types of organizations did not have a significant difference of perceptions when selecting AAM with the same qualifications over WM (see Table 8).

Table 8: Cross Tabulation of Type of Organization by Preference of Type of Candidates

| | *Type of Candidates* | | | | | |
| | Industry | | Commerce | | Service | |
	Count	%	Count	%	Count	%
African-American Managers	11	85	7	70	42	81
White Managers	2	15	3	30	10	19
Total	13	100	10	100	52	100

Chi-Square: 0.817, df = 2, p> 0.05

The experience variable was measured by items 9, 10, 24, and 25 from the questionnaire administered to the sample. A cross tabulation and a Chi-Square statistical analysis was performed between types of organizations and these four items separately. Results from the cross tabulation between items 9 and 24 and types of organizations showed a statistically significant difference. Item 9 showed a statistically significant difference in the perceptions of the AAM from different types of organizations regarding the experience in management in previous jobs. A Chi-Square value of 18.67 was found to be significant at an 0.05 alpha level of significance. The results (see Table 9) indicated that the highest percent of respondents from commerce and service (62 and 57% respectively) strongly agreed with this item when compared with industry (53%).

Table 9: Cross Tabulation of Type of Organization by Perception of Previous Jobs as Source of Experience in Management

| | Perceptions About AAM's Management Experience | | | | | |
| | Industry | | Commerce | | Service | |
	Count	%	Count	%	Count	%
Not sure	1	6	1	8	9	11
Strongly Disagree	1	6	3	23	10	12
Disagree	6	35	1	8	17	20
Agree	0	0	5	38	32	39
Strongly Agree	9	53	3	23	15	18
Total	17	100	13	100	83	100

Chi-Square: 18.67, df= 8, p< 0.05

Item twenty-four measured the perceptions of AAM regarding the experience to qualify for a managerial position, specifically if they believed that most of them had limited experience. Results from the cross tabulation between this item and types of organizations indicated a significant difference of opinion among the managers. The Chi-Square value found was 20.4 at an alpha level of 0.0088 (p < 0.05). While 69% of the commerce managers were grouped in the agree strongly agree categories, only 15% disagreed.

The networking variable was measured by items 11 and 17 from the questionnaire. No significant differences were found using the Chi-Square statistical analysis (p > 0.05). For item 11 a Chi-Square value of 9.20 was found (p > 0.05), which revealed that different types of organizations did not have significant different perceptions about the participation of AAM in professional network inside or out side their organizations. There was a high percent of agreement among the three types of managers about this issue (see Table 11).

Table 10: Cross tabulation of Type of Organization by Perception of Limited Experience in Management

| | *Perceptions About Limited Management Experience* | | | | | |
| | Industry | | Commerce | | Service | |
	Count	%	Count	%	Count	%
Not sure	0	0	2	15	2	2
Strongly Disagree	7	41	0	0	15	18
Disagree	3	18	2	15	30	36
Agree	2	12	2	15	18	21
Strongly Agree	5	29	7	55	19	23
Total	17	100	13	100	84	100

Chi-Square:20.44, df = 8, p < 0.05

disagreed. On the other hand, for each group in the industry and service managers, over 54% disagreed or strongly disagreed in their perceptions (see Table 10).

Table 11: Cross tabulation of Type of Organization by AAM Participation in Professional Network

| | *Perceptions About AAM Network Participation* | | | | | |
| | Industry | | Commerce | | Service | |
	Count	%	Count	%	Count	%
Not sure	0	0	2	15	2	2
Strongly Disagree	7	41	0	0	15	18
Disagree	3	18	2	15	30	36
Agree	2	12	2	15	18	21
Strongly Agree	5	29	7	55	19	23
Total	17	100	13	100	84	100

Chi-Square: 9.21, df = 8, p > 0.05

Further analysis of the perceptions regarding experience was measured by items 10 and 25. No significant difference were found using the Chi-Square statistical analysis (p > 0.05). Most of the managers in the three types of organizations agreed that the AAM obtained their experience in management through in house" training and that there were experienced AAM's interested in these positions.

Further analysis on perceptions of networking was measured by question 17 which asked if inappropriate professional networking was hindering AAM's access to managerial positions. The Chi-Square analysis revealed a non significant value of 5.60 (p> 0.05). This result indicated that different types of organizations did not have significant different perceptions regarding this item. As illustrated in Table 12, the opinions were widely spread among the different categories of the Likert Scale for this item. There was not a definite pattern of agreement in their opinions.

Table 12: Cross Tabulation of Type of Organization by Degree of Agreement in Inappropriate Professional Networking

	Perceptions About Inappropriate Networking					
	Industry		Commerce		Service	
	Count	%	Count	%	Count	%
Not sure	1	6	1	8	7	8
Strongly Disagree	5	29	1	8	12	14
Disagree	5	29	1	31	22	27
Agree	4	24	2	15	22	27
Strongly Agree	2	12	5	38	20	24
Total	17	100	10	100	83	100

Chi-Square: 5.60, df = 8, p > 0.05

It can be concluded that there was not a significant difference by types of organizations where networking was hindering AAM's access to managerial positions.

Job opportunities were measured by item 19 which asked if AAM job opportunities were equal to WM. When this item was analyzed by types of organizations a Chi-Square value of 9.79 was obtained. This value was found to be statistical non-significant at the C.05 alpha level of significance. This result indicated that there was no difference in the opinions of the three different types of managers regarding this item.

Research Question #2: This research question was formulated in order to determine if there was a significant difference between the perceptions of managers of organizations with affirmative action and incentive programs and the perception of those managers of those organizations without those programs regarding qualifications, networking, requirements and job opportunities. This question was analyzed cross tabulating the item in the questionnaire (item 5) referring to affirmative action program (yes or no) and the items referring to qualifications (item 6-7).

When asked if their firm's needs required academic qualifications that were present in AAM, the results were varied. The variable qualification was measured by items 6, 7, and 37. The cross tabulation analysis showed no significant difference in their opinions for the two groups for the three items that measured qualifications. For item 6, the results are summarized in Table 13.

Table 13: Cross tabulation and Chi-Square Analysis of Managers with Affirmative Action Programs vs Those Without Those Programs Regarding Qualification (Item 6)

| | Perceptions About Qualifications | | | |
| | Industry | | Commerce | |
	Count	%	Count	%
Not sure	1	2	2	3
Strongly Disagree	2	4	3	5
Disagree	5	10	9	15
Agree	8	15	15	24
Strongly Agree	36	69	33	53
Total	52	100	62	100

Chi-Square 3.08, df = 4 (p> 0.05)

These results showed that over 70% of the sample in the two groups agreed or strongly agreed in their opinions about the qualifications of Black managers.

When asked if AAM were qualified academically but exhibited a lack of other needed attributes to become managers, there were no significant differences in the opinions of those managers with affirmative action programs and those without the incentive programs. The cross tabulation analysis for this question (item 7) was not significant at the 0.05 alpha level of significance. What follows is a summary table for the cross tabulation analysis.

Table 14: Cross Tabulation of Managers with Affirmative Action Programs vs Those Without Those Programs Regarding Other Attributes (Item 7)

| | Perceptions About Other Needed Attributes | | | |
| | Industry | | Commerce | |
	Count	%	Count	%
Not sure	2	4	3	5
Strongly Disagree	16	30	15	25
Disagree	17	32	15	25
Agree	13	24	16	26
Strongly Agree	5	10	12	19
Total	105	100	123	100

Chi-Square: 3.00, df= 4 (p >0.05)

Results from Table 14 shows that there was a spread in the opinions from the two groups in the continuum of the Likert Scale.

The experience variable was measured by items 9, 10, 24, and 25 from the questionnaire administered to the sample. A cross tabulation and a Chi-Square statistical analysis was performed separately between the item that measured participation and no participation in Affirmative Action programs and these four items. Results from the cross tabulation between those items and item 5 (No Affirmative Action Programs – Affirmative Action Programs) showed no statistically significant difference. The opinions regarding these four items showed that both groups either agreed or strongly agreed with the opinions presented in these four items.

Respondents were asked to present their opinions to the item that asked if AAM obtained their experience in management in previous jobs. When the cross tabulation of this item with the participation - no participation in Affirmative Action programs was performed, the results showed a non-significant Chi Square value of 5.15. Table 15 summarizes the results for this cross tabulation.

Table 15: Cross Tabulation of Managers with Affirmative Actions Programs vs Those Without Those Programs Regarding Experience in Previous Jobs (Item 9)

| | *Perceptions About Previous Job Experience* | | | |
| | Industry | | Commerce | |
	Count	%	Count	%
Not sure	4	8	7	12
Strongly Disagree	9	17	6	10
Disagree	8	15	16	26
Agree	21	40	16	26
Strongly Agree	11	20	16	26
Total	53	100	61	100

Chi-Square 5.15, df = 4 (p > 0.05)

The results suggested that both groups had similar opinions regarding this issue and that this opinion was split between those who agreed or strongly agreed and those who disagreed or strongly disagreed.

Item 10 asked the sample to express their opinion regarding AAM's experience in management through "in house" training. The results of the analysis showed no significant difference in their opinions (Affirmative vs. Non Affirmative). The following table presents a summary of these results.

Table 16: Cross Tabulation of Managers with Affirmative Action Programs vs. Those Without Those Programs Regarding In House Training (Item 10)

| | Perceptions About In House Training | | | |
| | Industry | | Commerce | |
	Count	%	Count	%
Not sure	5	9	5	8
Strongly Disagree	4	8	6	10
Disagree	8	15	13	21
Agree	19	36	19	31
Strongly Agree	17	32	18	30
Total	53	100	61	100

Chi-Square: 1.06, df = 4 (p > 0.05)

Results from Table 16 showed that about 60's of the sample from both groups agreed or strongly agreed to this item, resulting in a non-significant difference in opinions.

Item 24 asked the respondents to present their opinions to the fact that since AAM's were recently entering into the work force, most of them have limited experience to qualify for a managerial position. The results of the cross tabulation of this item by item 5 (Affirmative vs. Non-Affirmative) showed a non-significant Chi-Square value of 1.04 (p > 0.05). The following table presents a summary of these results.

Table 17: Cross Tabulation Analysis of Managers with Affirmative Action Programs vs. Those Without Those Program Regarding Limited Experience for Managerial Position (Item 24)

| | Perceptions About Limited Experience | | | |
| | Industry | | Commerce | |
	Count	%	Count	%
Not sure	2	4	2	3
Strongly Disagree	10	19	11	18
Disagree	18	34	19	31
Agree	8	15	14	23
Strongly Agree	15	28	16	24
Total	53	100	62	100

Chi-Square: 3.08, df = 4 (p > 0.05)

Table 17 illustrates that the two groups' perceptions were almost consistent to one another regarding this item along the five categories of the scale.

The sample was asked to answer if there were experienced AAM interested in managerial positions at the moment the organizations were recruiting. The cross tabulation of this item by item 5 (Affirmative vs. Non-Affirmative Action Programs) showed that there were no significant differences in the opinions of the two groups regarding this item. A Chi-Square value of 2.69 was found (p > 0.05). Table 18 presents a summary of these results.

Table 18: Cross Tabulation of Managers with Affirmative Action Programs vs Those Without those Programs Regarding Experienced AAM Interested in Managerial Positions at Time of Recruitment (Item 25)

	Perceptions About Experience at Time of Recruitment			
	Industry		Commerce	
	Count	%	Count	%
Not sure	9	17	5	8
Strongly Disagree	5	9	5	8
Disagree	10	19	14	24
Agree	15	28	16	26
Strongly Agree	14	27	2].	34
Total	53	100	61	100

Chi-Square 2.69, df = 4 (P > 0.05)

The results indicated in Table 18 reflect that the opinions of the two groups were similar along the scale for this item.

Regarding the networking variable, as measured by items 11 and 17, no significant difference was found in the perceptions of those managers with Affirmative Action Programs and those without the programs. The Chi-Square analysis showed no significant value at the 0.05 level of significance. The opinions were varied and no consistent pattern of opinions were found. There was a wide spread of opinions along the continuum of the Likert Scale.

For item 11 a Chi-Square value of 2.30 was found (p > 0.05), which indicated that managers with Affirmative Action Programs did not differ from those without the programs in their opinions about the participation of AAM is professional network inside or outside their organizations. Their opinions were widely spread across the different categories of the Likert Scale used (See Table 19).

Table 19: Cross Tabulation of Managers with Affirmative Action Programs vs. Those Without Those Programs Regarding Networking (Item 11)

	Perceptions About Networking			
	Industry		Commerce	
	Count	%	Count	%
Not sure	1	2	2	3
Strongly Disagree	2	4	3	5
Disagree	5	10	9	1
Agree	8	15	15	24
Strongly Agree	36	69	33	53
Total	52	100	62	100

Chi-square: 3.08, df = 4(p > 0.05)

The other networking variable was measured by Item 17 which asked if inappropriate professional networking was hindering AAM access to managerial positions. When the responses to this item were cross tabulated against Item 5, no significant differences were observed between the two groups (Affirmative vs. Non Affirmative Programs). A Chi-Square value of 2.53 showed no statistical significance (p >0.05). What follows is a summary table 20 for this item.

Table 20: Cross Tabulation of Managers with Affirmative Action Programs vs. Those Without Those Programs Regarding Inappropriate Professional Networking Hindering Access to Managerial Position (Item 17)

	Perceptions About Inappropriate Networking			
	Industry		Commerce	
	Count	%	Count	%
Not sure	5	9	3	5
Strongly Disagree	8	15	10	16
Disagree	17	32	16	26
Agree	10	19	18	30
Strongly Agree	13	25	14	23
Total	53	100	61	100

Chi-Square 2.53, df = 4 (p > 0.05)

Table 20 shows that the opinions were divided evenly among the four major categories of the scale (strongly disagree to strongly agree). The percentages in the cell for the two groups were very similar indicating that their is no difference in their opinions regarding this item.

Job opportunities were measured by Item 19 which asked if AAM job opportunities were equal to WM. The answers given by the sample to this item were analyzed and cross tabulated with the item that classified the organizations with Affirmative Action Programs versus those who did not have the programs. Results of this analysis showed that there was no difference in the opinions of the two groups with respect to this item. A Chi-Square value of 5.15 was found to be non-significant at an alpha level of significance of 0.05. Table 21 illustrates a summary of these findings.

Table 21: Cross Tabulation of Managers with Affirmative Action Programs vs. Those Without Those Program Regarding Job Opportunities (Item 19)

	Perceptions About Job Opportunities			
	Industry		Commerce	
	Count	%	Count	%
Not sure	4	8	7	12
Strongly Disagree	9	17	6	10
Disagree	8	15	16	26
Agree -	21	40	16	26
Strongly Agree	11	20	16	26
Total	53	100	61	100

Chi-Square 5.15, df = 4 (p > 0.05)

Responses given to this item by the two groups on the sample indicated that their opinions were almost the same for each one of the categories for the item. Similar percentages could be seen in the cells.

When the sample was divided into two groups using the Affirmative Action Program, no significant differences were observed in any of the variables studied between the two groups.

Research Question #3: This research question focused on the overall perceptions of respondents regarding African-American managers' career development and job opportunities. The analytical approach to help answer this question was to cross tabulate Items 28 through 31 with Item 1 from the questionnaire. This analysis provided a view of the opinions of the managers from the major categories from the three organizations; commerce, service, and industry.

When Item 1 (Type of Organization) was cross tabulated with Item 28, which asked if WM preferred to work with WM because they had the same management styles, a non-significant Chi-Square value was found. The following table shows the results from this analysis.

Table 22: Cross Tabulation of Type of Organization by WM Preference of Management Styles (Item 28)

	Perceptions About Preference of Management Styles					
	Industry		Commerce		Service	
	Count	%	Count	%	Count	%
Not sure	2	12	3	23	12	15
Strongly Disagree	4	24	1	8	10	12
Disagree	1	6	4	31	16	29
Agree	4	24	2	15	23	27
Strongly Agree	6	34	3	23	23	27
Total	17	100	13	100	84	100

Chi-Square:6.15, df = 8, p > 0.05

The results from Table 22 showed that, even though the opinions demonstrated no statistically significant difference, a high percentage (23%) of the managers from the commerce organizations were not sure about their opinions about the issue. Also, on the other side of the scale (Strongly Agree-Agree) they had the lowest percentage (38%) compared to 58% for industry and 54% for service.

Item 29 asked if African-American Managers preferred to work with AAM because they had the same management style. This item was cross tabulated with Item 1 (Types of Organizations). Results from this analysis showed that when asked if African-Americans preferred to work with African-Americans because they had the same management style, a significant difference was found using a Chi-Square statistic. A value of 17.51 was found to be significant at an alpha level of 0.05. Table 23 presents the results of such analysis.

Table 23: Cross Tabulation Type of Organizations by AAM Preference of Management Styles (Item 29)

| | Perceptions About Preference of Management Styles | | | | | |
| | Industry | | Commerce | | Service | |
	Count	%	Count	%	Count	%
Not sure	0	0	3	23	8	10
Strongly Disagree	10	59	1	8	17	20
Disagree	4	24	6	46	29	35
Agree	1	6	2	15	18	22
Strongly Agree	2	11	1	8	11	13
Total	17	100	13	100	83	100

Chi-Square: 17.51, df = 8, (p < 0.05)

The results in Table 23, indicated that there was a difference in the opinions of other subjects from the three different organizations. A great majority of industry managers (83%) disagreed or strongly disagreed. Commerce and service management opinions were split between agreement and disagreement on this issue.

Item 30 asked AAM to present their opinions regarding the characteristics that were promoting AAM's career development indicators. The item was cross tabulated with Item 1 (Types of Organizations). No statistically significant differences were found among the managers of the different types of organizations and the characteristics indicated in Item 30. All the Chi-Square values were found to be non-significant at the 0.05 alpha level.

Table 24: Chi-Square Values for AAM's Career Development Indicators of Item 30

| | Indicator | |
	Chi-Square	p Value
Promotion of incentive mechanisms	9.02*	34
Legal requirement and laws	4.09*	.85
Increased number of educated AAM	8.67*	34
Managing diversity techniques	6.76*	.56
Awareness of management styles	6.12*	.63
Corporate social responsibility	5.73*	.68
Shortage of qualified AAM	7.89*	.44

* (p > 0.05)

The respondents were asked to rate their opinions in a Likert scale regarding the characteristics that were hindering AAM in their career development. Twenty characteristics were cross tabulated by Item 1 (Types of Organizations). Out of those 20, only 9 Chi-Square values were found to be at the 0.05 significant level. Results were presented for significant values and a table will summarize the non-significant findings.

The first characteristic found to show differences in the opinions from the members of the three different organizations was that lack of confidence was hindering a career development. A Chi-Square value of 21.61 was found to be significant at the 0.05 alpha level. Table 25 shows these results.

Table 25: Cross Tabulation of Type of Organizations by Lack of Confidence

| | Perceptions About Confidence | | | | | |
| | Industry | | Commerce | | Service | |
	Count	%	Count	%	Count	%
Not sure	0	0	3	23	3	4
Strongly Disagree	6	38	1	8	12	16
Disagree	1	6	3	23	18	24
Agree	6	38	4	31	11	15
Strongly Agree	3	18	2	15	30	41
Total	16	100	13	100	74	100

Chi-Square 21.61, df = 8, (p < 0.05)

Lack of discipline was the next characteristic that showed significant differences when it was cross tabulated by type of organization. The Chi-Square value was 28.74 (p < 0.05). Table 26 shows the results of the analysis.

Table 26: Cross Tabulation of Type of Organization by Lack of Discipline

| | Perceptions About Discipline | | | | | |
| | Industry | | Commerce | | Service | |
	Count	%	Count	%	Count	%
Not sure	0	0	4	31	1	1
Strongly Disagree	5	31	3	23	18	23
Disagree	1	6	4	31	18	23
Agree	6	38	0	0	22	30
Strongly Agree	4	25	2	15	18	23
Total	16	100	13	100	77	100

Chi-Square: 28.74, df = 8 (p < 0.05)

These results showed that there was a significant difference between industry and service versus commerce. They agreed and strongly agreed that lack of confidence was hindering AAM in their career development. Managers from the commerce organizations disagreed and strongly disagreed regarding this item.

Insufficient education was the next characteristic in which the opinions from the members of the three types of organizations varied. Again the managers from service (53%) and industry (53%) agreed and strongly agreed that insufficient education was hindering AAM in their career development. Managers from commerce organizations disagreed and strongly disagreed (54%) from the other two organizations regarding this item. The Chi-Square value was 20.7 (p < .05). Table 27 summarizes these results.

Table 27: Cross Tabulation of Type of Organization by Insufficient Education

	Perceptions About Insufficient Education					
	Industry		Commerce		Service	
	Count	%	Count	%	Count	%
Not sure	0	0	3	25	1	1
Strongly Disagree	6	40	3	25	19	24
Disagree	1	7	3	25	16	21
Agree	3	20	1	8	19	24
Strongly Agree	5	33	2	17	23	30
Total	15	100	12	100	78	100

Chi-Square: 20. 7, df = 8 (p < 0.05)

The lack of technical and administrative skills was another characteristic that showed significant differences of opinions among the members of the three organizations. A Chi-Square value of 15.67 was found to be significant at 0.05 alpha level of significance. The main differences were found among the commerce and industry groups. The members of commerce organizations disagreed and strongly agreed (626). The members of services organization split almost half and half with respect to their opinion in this item. Results are presented in Table 28.

Table 28: Cross Tabulation of Type of Organization by Lack of Technical and Administrative Skills

	Perceptions About Skills					
	Industry		Commerce		Service	
	Count	%	Count	%	Count	%
Not sure	0	0	3	25	1	1
Strongly Disagree	5	31	3	25	19	24
Disagree	1	6	3	25	16	21
Agree	4	25	1	8	19	24
Strongly Agree	6	38	2	23	30	30
Total	16	100	12	78	100	100

Chi-Square:15.67, df = 8 (p < 0.05)

Another characteristic in which the opinions differed was lack of decision making styles. The significant difference regarding this item indicated that commerce disagreed and strongly disagreed that this characteristic was hindering AAM in their career development (50%). Industry and service managers agreed and strongly agreed that lack of decision making skills was hindering AAM in their career development (53% and 54% respectively). That difference in opinions was found to be significantly different at the .05 level. Table 29 presents these results.

Table 29: Cross tabulation of Type of Organization by Decision Making Styles

| | *Perceptions About Decision Making Styles* | | | | | |
| | Industry | | Commerce | | Service | |
	Count	%	Count	%	Count	%
Not sure	0	0	3	25	1	1
Strongly Disagree	6	40	3	25	19	24
Disagree	1	7	3	25	16	21
Agree	3	20	1	8	19	24
Strongly Agree	5	33	2	17	23	30
Total	15	100	12	100	78	100

Chi-Square:15.9, df = 8 (p< 0.05)

Regarding lack of time management skills, a significant difference was found regarding the opinions of the three different organizations' managers. A significant 17.9 Chi-Square value indicated that the managers from industry and service agreed and strongly agreed with this item. The responses showed that 81% of the industry managers agreed with this item. Fifty-seven of the managers from commerce disagreed with respect to this characteristic. Table 30 summarizes the results for the cross tabulation of this item with item 1.

Table 30: Cross Tabulation of Type of Organization by Lack of Time Management Skills

| | *Perceptions About Time Management Skills* | | | | | |
| | Industry | | Commerce | | Service | |
	Count	%	Count	%	Count	%
Not sure	0	0	2	17	2	2
Strongly Disagree	2	12	3	25	12	15
Disagree	1	6	3	25	21	26
Agree	6	38	1	8	19	24
Strongly Agree	7	44	3	25	26	33
Total	16	100	12	100	80	100

Chi-Square:17.9, df = 8 (p < 0.05)

Lack of experience was the next characteristics that showed significant differences in the opinions of the members of the three groups. A Chi-Square value of 21.8 was found significant at the 0.05 alpha level. Regarding this item, the industry members disagreed and strongly disagreed (54%). Commerce and services members agreed and strongly agreed with this as a characteristic that was hindering AAM in their career development (59% and 62% respectively). Table 31 present a summary of the results.

49

Table 31: Cross Tabulation of Type of Organization by Lack of Experience

	Perceptions About Lack of Experience					
	Industry		Commerce		Service	
	Count	%	Count	%	Count	%
Not sure	0	0	3	25	4	5
Strongly Disagree	7	47	0	0	9	12
Disagree	1	7	2	16	17	22
Agree	4	26	4	34	22	29
Strongly Agree	3	20	3	25	25	33
Total	15	100	12	100	77	100

Chi-Square: 21.7, df = 8 (p< 0.05)

Another characteristic that showed significant differences in opinions among the members of the three organizations was jealousy of AAM and peers with a Chi Square of 16.7.

The members of Service agreed and strongly agreed with this item (59%). Members from Industry and Commerce disagreed and strongly disagreed with the item (53% and 50%). Table 32 presents the results.

Table 32: Cross Tabulation of Type of Organization by Jealousy of AAM and Peers

	Perceptions About Jealousy					
	Industry		Commerce		Service	
	Count	%	Count	%	Count	%
Not sure	1	7	3	25	4	8
Strongly Disagree	5	33	0	0	14	19
Disagree	3	20	6	50	11	15
Agree	3	20	2	17	21	28
Strongly Agree	3	20	1	8	23	31
Total	15	100	12	100	73	100

Chi-Square:16.7, df = 8 (p < 0.05)

When asked if AAM's preference for traditional roles as mediators, harmonizers and pacifiers was hindering AAM in their career development, a significant difference was shown regarding the opinions of the members of the three organizations with a Chi-Square of 17.2. The members of the Commerce organizations disagreed and strongly disagreed with this position (66%). The Industry and Service members agreed or strongly agreed with this item (56% and 55%). Table 33 present a summary of the results.

**Table 33: Cross Tabulation of Type of Organization
by AAM's Preference for Traditional Roles**

	Perceptions About Traditional Roles					
	Industry		Commerce		Service	
	Count	%	Count	%	Count	%
Not sure	0	0	1	8	6	8
Strongly Disagree	3	19	4	33	14	18
Disagree	4	25	4	33	14	18
Agree	7	44	2	17	16	21
Strongly Agree	2	13	1	8	27	35
Total	16	100	12	100	77	100

Chi-Square:17.2, df = 8 (p< 0.05)

Eleven of the twenty characteristics showed no significant differences among the three types of organizations. Table 34 summarizes the results for these items.

**Table 34: Summary of Chi-Square Values for
Factors Hindering AAM in Their Career Development**

Factors	Chi-Square Value	p Value
Lack of emotional control	11.92	0.15
Difficulty in handling pressure	14.89	0.06
Excessively aggressive	14.51	0.07
Lack of aggressiveness	14.20	0.08
Inadequate communication skills	14.24	0.08
Insufficient human relation skills	13.7	0.09
Rivalry of WM and peers	7.78	0.46
Aversion to relocate	10.97	0.20
Don't want to work long hours or unusual schedule	6.14	0.63
Excessively outspoken	8.81	0.36

Research Question #4: This research question asked the respondents to rate the overall evaluation regarding African-American managers' level of satisfaction, productivity and job quality, managerial styles and managerial skills. To help answer this question cross tabulations were performed for items 32 - 35 and item 1 (Types of Organizations).

When asked about the level of satisfaction with the white managers, no significant differences were found in the sample between them members of the three organizations (commerce, industry, and service). A Chi-Square value of 3.57 was found to non-significant at the 0.05 alpha level. The responses in the different categories followed a similar pattern for the three groups.

Similar results were obtained when they were asked to rate their level of satisfaction with African-American managers. No significant differences were found. A Chi Square value of

6.96 showed no significance at the 0.05 alpha level. A similar pattern of responses was shown or the three groups (from extremely satisfied to not at all satisfied)

Regarding the rating of AAM in terms of productivity and job quality, no significant differences were found. A Chi-Square value of 1.64 proved to be non-significant ($p > 0.05$). The results indicated that there were no significant differences in the opinions of the three groups.

Item 34, which asked the opinions about A1 managerial styles showed significant differences among the three groups. Commerce and Industry managers believed that the managerial styles of AAM were somewhat different from white managers. The members of Service believed that the managerial styles of AAM were very different from those managers. A Chi-Square value of 9.74 was significant at the 0.05 level of significance. Table 35 presents the results of findings.

Table 35: Cross Tabulation of Type of Organization by Opinions of Managerial Styles

	Perceptions About Managerial Styles					
	Industry		Commerce		Service	
	Count	%	Count	%	Count	%
Same style	4	25	3	25	11	16
Very different	4	25	0	0	31	44
Somewhat different	8	50	9	75	29	40
Total	16	100	12	100	71	100

Chi-Square:9.74, df = 4 ($p < 0.05$)

No significant differences were found between the managers from the three types of organizations regarding their opinions on which skills AAMs perform better. A nonsignificant Chi-square value was found at the 0.05 alpha level. Their opinions were varied among the three alternatives: technical skills, human skills, and conceptual skills. Even though no significant differences were found, the Commerce managers would prefer candidates with human skills. Industry managers would prefer candidates with technical skills.

Research Question #5: This research question asked the organizations' projects regarding African-American Managerial positions. Cross tabulations were performed between items 36 and 37 with item 1. When asked about how many managerial positions would open in the near future, no significant differences were found among the managers from the three organizations.

Respondents were asked that if they were to decide among two individuals of different gender with the same qualifications which one would they select. No significant differences were found. The preference was unanimously for African-American managers. Over 70% of them selected the AAM category over the WM category. Table 36 presents the results of this item.

Table 36: Cross Tabulation of Type of Organization Preference (Item 37)

| | Perceptions About Preference | | | | | |
| | Industry | | Commerce | | Service | |
	Count	%	Count	%	Count	%
African-American Managers	11	85	7	70	42	81
White Managers	2	15	3	30	10	19
Total	13	100	10	100	52	100

Research Question #6: This research question asked the respondents to rank the factors that may affect AAM's access in top managerial positions in government and private companies in order of importance. The criteria used for his analysis was the percent of obtained by each category. Experience was chosen as the most important factor for the members of the three organizations. The second most important factor was background. Reduction of AAM participation in the work force was chosen as the third most important factor. Cultural and social patterns were the next most important followed by leadership characteristics. There were some missing information regarding this question and the respondents did not rate all the criteria presented in the item.

**Table 37: Rank Ordering
of Factors Affecting AAM Access to Managerial Positions**

Factor	Rank
Experience	1
Background	2
Reduction of AAM participation in work force	3
Cultural and social patterns	4
Leadership characteristics	5

The analysis of the data gathered in this study enabled this researcher to discern and examine the perceptions of AAM about factors that impact their career development and job opportunities. The outcomes facilitated this by reaching conclusions which illustrated the profile of the particular population studied.

The conclusions, implications and recommendations that resulted from the analysis of the findings of this study are presented in Chapter V.

Chapter
5

Conclusions, Implications and Recommendations

This study was intended to determine the African-American Managers' perceptions about factors that impact their career development and job opportunities. The theoretical framework, outlined by various researchers related to the outcomes of this study support the conclusions, implications, and recommendations presented in this chapter.

CONCLUSIONS

In light of the analysis of the data gathered, the researcher concluded the following:

1. AAM perceived that their present firms' needs required academically qualified professionals.
2. There was not a consistent pattern regarding AAM's academic qualifications and lack of needed attributes to become good managers.
3. Managers in commerce considered that AAMs have limited experience to qualify for a managerial position while managers in industry did not agree with this position.
4. Managers concurred that AAM were part of a professional network inside or outside their organizations, but inappropriate networking hindered their access to managerial positions.
5. There was not a significant pattern of opinions regarding AAM's job opportunities.
6. AAM of organizations with Affirmative Actions Programs and AAM of organizations without those programs considered that their firms' needs required academic qualifications that were present in AAM.
7. AAM's career development and opportunities were hindered by lack of confidence and discipline, insufficient education, time, management, technical and administrative skills, decision making styles, and preferences for traditional roles as mediators, harmonizers, and pacifiers.
8. Commerce managers preferred candidates with human skills while industry managers preferred those with technical skills.
9. AAM preferred to hire Black Americans for management positions.
10. Factors that affected the access of AAM to top managerial positions in the future were the following in the order of precedence: experience, background, reduction of AAM's participation in the work force, cultural and social patterns, and leadership characteristics.

IMPLICATIONS

The implications of the study could be directed toward social change. The world needs to identify and correct barriers that impede AAM's full utilization, and capabilities in today's society. It is urgent to the State of Illinois to utilize human resources to a maximum. Recent research has identified AAM's as a most valuable human resource in the State of Illinois

(Central Management System in the State of Illinois, 1990). Its necessary to utilize their capabilities to the maximum. Capable individuals should receive the same opportunity to exert their full potential, independently of managerial style. Since cultural factors may be influencing the neglected utilization of AAM for managerial positions, it is necessary (1) to identify the existing problems; and (2) to suggest possible alternatives to eradicate or diminish the problems. It is essential to recognize that there are limited differences between top managers and AAM, with neither management being superior over the other (Macionies, 1991). It will be necessary to deal with perceptions, or preconceived ideas, formed over time through formal and informal social processes, culture, networking, diversity, technical, and administrative skills, that may affect human behavior in the decision making process. It will be necessary to use formal and informal education to accomplish their goal. This process should be directed to all of the Illinois business population.

The educational system must be revised in order to develop new concepts in young AAM in the State of Illinois' future. Top managers need to perceive the new AAM's role for the global economy. A study prepared by Sorrel (1989), evaluates the concept AAM have of themselves. This is considered a decisive factors in impeding career development. This study confirms that AAM identify themselves in positions in society and begin their selection for a future profession. AAM are conditioned to specific patterns that describe their role and establish limitations in their development. They receive social role modeling that limits their ambitions and motivations. For AAM's to have a competitive future their mentality for new concepts and desirable characteristics must be prepared. AAM's mentality should be oriented to the business where they and top managers have the same opportunities.

During the last decades, AAM developed desirable characteristics to triumph in business. The desirable characteristics for successful individual includes: courage, self-satisfaction, vitality, perseverance, organization, open mindedness, equilibrium, and ambition (Hockenmack, 1972).

Current managers' perceptions toward AAM professional networking seems to be negative. Notwithstanding, if AAM professional organizations promote publicly their accomplishments, they will improve their perceptions. More important, AAM should increase their participation in top management professional organizations to affirm they are part of the same professional group.

Since AAM are entering recently in management, they have to "pay the price" of being short of experience. However, these perceptions do not seem to be affecting severely their management development. Strong managers' perceptions reflect that AAM cannot apply the same effort to their career as the top managers do. Since a high percentage of these perceptions correspond to the traditional AAM role in business, social changes may be needed. It is imminent to reeducate society regarding AAM's role. The Illinois business environment has to be understood as a working place, where everyone needs to cooperate. AAM have to learn this with their communities and internalize and carry it for the future, this way they will be changing the existing traditional AAM role.

Social changes regarding the present situation with incentives for managerial participation are necessary. It is evident that voluntary incentives that promote their access to management are not existing. Professional, private and government institutions may encourage their use and give recognition to AAM businesses. Since legal requirements are considered as a reason that has promoting AAM in their management advancement, governmental monitoring may be enforced in this area. Government involvement is imperative. AAM career development must be stimulated and utilization of human resources in all areas of economy, at all levels, including management, must be the object of incentive and legal enforcement.

RECOMMENDATIONS

Based on the analysis of the findings, conclusions, and implications of this study, the following recommendations are presented:

1. Industry, commerce, service and government organizations should develop and awareness of the needs of AAM in order to secure more participation of this sector of society in career development and job opportunities.

2. A plan of action should to be created focus on all factors that affect AAM's participation of this sector of society in career development and job opportunities.

3. Additional analysis should be conducted to determine the extent to which individual AAM who need and desire a particular training or service can get it.

4. Follow-up studies should be done with the purpose of validating the AAM's perceptions about factors that impact their career development and job opportunities.

5. AAM's participation in professional, private, civic, state, and national government organizations should be promoted at all levels.

6. An educational system of encouragement for AAM to compete for excellence should be implemented.

Bibliography

Alderfer, C. P. (1972). Existence, relatedness and growth. New York: Free Press.

Anastasi, A. (1989). Ability testing in the 1980's and beyond. Public Personnel Management. 19, 471-484.

Anderson, M. B., & Iwanicki, E. F. (1984). Teacher motivation and its relationship to burnout. Educational Administration Quarterly, 20, 109-132.

Argyris, C. (1957). Personality and the organization. New York: Harper and Row.

Armstrong, T. R., Chalupsky, A. B., McLaughlin, D. H., & Dalldorf, M. R. (1988). Armed Services Vocational Aptitude Battery Validation for civilian occupations. Brook Air Force Base, TX: Air Force Human Resources.

Asante, M. K. (1987). The afro centric idea. Philadelphia: Temple University Press.

Ash, P., Slora, K. & Britton, C. (1990). Policy agency officer selection practices. Journal of Police Science Administration, 17, 258-269.

Austin, J. T., & Hanisch, K. A. (   ). Occupational attainment as a function of abilities and interests: A longitudinal analysis using project TALENT data. Journal of Applied Psychology, 75, 77-86.

Beane, J. A. (1990). Self-concept self-esteem and the curriculum. New York: Teachers College Press.

Best, J. W. (1981). Research in education. Englewood Cliffs, NJ: Prentice-Hall.

Biklin, S. K., & Branningan, M. (1980). Women and educational leadership. Lexington, MA: Heath.

Billard, M. (1992, March). Do women make better managers? Working Woman, 68-71.

Bohlman, L. G. (1985). Modern approaches to understanding and managing organizations. San Francisco: Jossey-Bass.

Borg, W. R. & Gall, M. D. (1983). Educational research: An introduction. New York: Longman.

Campion, M. A. (1989). Ability requirement implications of job design: An interdisciplinary perspective. Personnel Psychology, 42, 1-24.

Census of Population Housing. (1990). Washington, D.C.: U.S. Government Printing Office.

Colberg, M. (1985). Logic-based measurement of verbal reasoning: A key to increased validity and economy. Personnel Psychology. 38, 357-359.

Combs, A. W. & Snygg, D. (1959). Individual behavior: A perceptual approach to behavior. New York: Longman.

Dow, M. (1992, November). Power. Working Woman, 98-99.

Drew, C. J. (1980). Introduction to designing and conducting research. Utah: The C. V. Mosby Co.

Drucker, P. (1982). The changing world of the executive. New York: New York Times Books.

Fagenson, E. D. (1989). At the heart of women in management research: Theoretical and methodological approaches. Journal of Business Ethics, 9, 367-374.

Fowler, F., Jr. (1988). Survey research methods Beverly Hills, CA: Sage Publications.

Gardner, D. G. & Discenza, R. (1988). Sex effects in evaluating applicant qualifications: A re-examination. <u>Sex Roles</u>, 18, 297-308.

Garibaldi, A. M. (1992). Educating and motivating African-American males to succeed. <u>Journal of Negro Education</u>, 61 (1) 4-11.

Garland, S. B. (1991, September 2). How to keep women on the corporate ladder. <u>Business Week</u>, 64.

Gibson, E. J. (1969). <u>Principles of perceptual learning and development.</u> New York: Appleton-CenturyCrofts.

Gilliland, H. (1988). <u>Teaching the Native American.</u> Dubuque, IA: Kendall/Hunt.

Glasser, W. (1965). <u>Reality therapy.</u> New York: Harper & Row.

Gordon, J. R. (1983). <u>A diagnostic approach to organizational behavior.</u> Boston: Allyn and Bacon.

Graves, L. M. & Powerll, G. N. (1988). An investigation of sex discrimination in recruiters' evaluation. <u>Journal of Applied Psychology</u>, 73, 20-29.

Hackamack, L. C., & Solid, A. B. (1972, April). The woman executive. <u>Business Horizons</u>.

Hammer, E. G. & Kleiman, L. A. (1988). Getting to know you. <u>Personnel Administration</u>, 34, 86-92.

Harris, M. M. (1989). Reconsidering the employment interview: A review of recent literature and suggestions for future research. <u>Personnel Psychology</u>, 42, 691-726.

Heilman, M. E. & Hornstein, H. A. (1982). <u>Managing human forces in organizations.</u> Homewood, IL: Richard D. Irwin.

Hersey, P., et al. (1988). <u>Management of organizational behavior.</u> Englewood Cliffs, NJ: PrenticeHall.

Herzberg, F. (1966). <u>Work and the nature of man.</u> Cleveland: World.

Herzberg, F. (1987). One more time: How do you motivate employees? <u>Harvard Business Review, 65,</u> 112.

Holt, D. H. (1990). <u>Management.</u> Englewood Cliffs, NJ: Prentice-Hall.

Honeman, B. (1990). <u>Rational and suggestions for emphasizing Afrocentricity in the public schools.</u> Paper presented at the Conference on Rhetoric and Teaching of Writing, Indiana, PA.

Hunter, J. E. (1986). Cognitive ability, cognitive aptitudes, job knowledge, and job performance. <u>Journal of Vocational Behavior</u>, 29, 840-862.

Hunter, J. E. & Schmidt, F. L. (1990a). <u>Methods of meta-analysis Correcting error and bias in research findings.</u> Newbury Park, CA: Sage Publications.

Jensen, A. IL (1986). G: Artifact or reality? <u>Vocational Behavior.</u> 29, 301-331.

Jones, M. et. al. (1988). <u>Inside organizations.</u> Beverly Hills, CA: Sage Publications.

Kanter, R. M. (1977). <u>Men of the corporation.</u> New York: Basic Books.

Koretz, G. (1992, January 27). America's neglected weapon: Its educated women. <u>Business Week</u>, 22.

Kossen, S. (1991). <u>The human side of organizations.</u> New York: Harper-Collins.

Leedy, P. D. (1985). <u>Practical research planning and design.</u> New York: Macmillan.

Lengerman, P. M. & Wallace, R. A. (1985). <u>Gender in America Social control and social change.</u> Englewood Cliffs, NJ: Prentice-Hall.

Lewis, L. (1985). <u>The motivating leader.</u> Englewood Cliffs, NJ: Prentice-Hall.

Lunenburg, F. C. & Ornstein, A. C. (1991). <u>Educational administration Concepts and practices.</u> Belmont, CA: Wadsworth.

Macionis, J. J. (1991). <u>Sociology.</u> Englewood Cliffs, NJ: Prentice-Hall.

Martin, C. L. & Nagao, D. H. (1989). Some effects of computerized interviewing on job applicant responses. <u>Journal of Aptlied Psychology,</u> 75, 72-80.

Maslow, A. H. (1970). <u>Motivation and personality.</u> New York: Cambridge University Press.

McClelland, D. C. (1988). <u>Human motivation.</u> New York: Cambridge University Press.

Mead, G. H. (1964). <u>On social psychology.</u> Chicago: University of Chicago Press.

Merriam, S. B. (1989). <u>A guide to research for educators and trainers of adults.</u> Florida: Robert E. Kreiger.

Mertzger, W. (1976). <u>Los prejuicios.</u> Barcelona: Editorial Herder. Naisbitt, J., & Aburdene, P. (1990). Megatrends 2000, New York: Morrow.

Naisbitt, J., & Aburdene, P. (1990). <u>Megatrends 2000.</u> New York: Morrow

Niereriberg, J. (1993). <u>The living organization Transformation teams into workplace communities.</u> San Diego: Business One Irwin Homewood.

Obiakor, F. E. (1991, February). <u>Crisis in the education of minorities.</u> Paper presented at the Multicultural Fair, University of Tennessee, Chattanooga, TN.

Office of the Assistant Secretary of Defense, Force Management and Personnel. (1990). <u>Report to the House on appropriations joint-services efforts to link enlistment standards to job performance.</u> Washington, DC: Office of Assistant Secretary of Defense (p. 33).

O'Sullivan, R. G. & Barber, C. R. (1991, April). <u>Evaluation of school incentive teams.</u> Paper presented at the annual meeting of the American Educational Research Association, Chicago, IL.

Palmer, M. (1990). <u>Women in management: Developing the skills that work.</u> New York: AMA Extension Institute.

Piaget, M. (1954). <u>The construction of reality in the Child.</u> New York: Basic Brooks.

Porter, L. W., et al. (1975). <u>Behavior in organizations.</u> New York: McGraw-Hill.

Power, G. N. (1990, August). One more time: Do female and male managers differ? <u>Academy of Management Executive,</u> 48-54.

Prediger, D. J. (1989). Ability differences across occupations: More than g. <u>Journal of Vocational Behavior,</u> 34, 1-27.

Prior, D. W., et. al. (1991). Teaching decision-making using situational leadership. <u>Journal of Creative Behavior,</u> 34, 1-27.

Raymond, H. A. (1986). <u>Management in the third wave.</u> Glenview, IL: Scott Foresman.

Robbins, S. p. (1991). <u>Organizational behavior.</u> Englewood Cliffs, NJ: Prentice-Hall.

Russell, C. J. (1990). Selecting top corporate leaders: An example of biographical information. <u>Journal of Management,</u> 16, 73-86.

Schmidt, F. L., Hunter, J. E., Outerbridge, A. N., & Goff, S. (1988b). Joint relation of experience and ability with job performance: Test of three hypotheses. <u>Journal of Applied Psychology,</u> 43, 617-670.

Sergiovanni, T. J. (1989). Science and scientism in supervision and teaching. <u>Journal of Curriculum and Supervision</u> 4(2), 93-105.

Sinclair, R. L. & Ghorty, W. J. (1987). <u>Reaching marginal students A primary concern for school renewal.</u> New York: McCutchan.

Slavin, R. E., et al. (1990). <u>Effective programs for students at risk.</u> Boston: Allyn & Bacon.

Sowell, T. (1989, December). Affirmative action: A world-wide disaster. <u>Commentary,</u> 21-41.

Spencer, J. M. (1989). When preferential hiring becomes reverse discrimination. <u>Employment Relations,</u> 14, 13-29.

Szilagyi, A. D., Jr. & Wallace, M. J., Jr. (1993) <u>Organizational behavior and performance</u> (5th ed.). Glenview: Scott, Foresman & Co.

Thorndike, R. L. (1986). The role of general ability in prediction. <u>Journal of Vocational Behavior,</u> 29, 332339.

Toffler, A. (1990). <u>Powers shift.</u> New York: Bantam Books.

Warner, R. L. & Steele, B. 5. (1989). Affirmative action in times of fiscal stress and changing value priorities: A case of women in policing. <u>Public Personnel Management Journal,</u> 18, 291-309.

Weisner, W. H. & Cronshaw, S. F. (1988). A meta-analytic investigation of the impact of interview format and degree of structure on the validity of the employment interview. <u>Journal of Occupational Psychology,</u> 61, 275-290.

Welsh, J. R., Kucinkas, S. K., & Curran, L. T. (1990). <u>Armed Services Vocational Battery (ASVABL Predicting military criteria from general and specific abilities.</u> Brooks Air Force Base, TX: Air Force Human Resources Laboratory.

Wright, P. M., Lichtenfels, P. A., & Pursell, E. D. (1989). The structured interview: Additional studies and a meta-analysis. <u>Journal of occupational Psychology,</u> 62, 191-199.

Appendix

QUESTIONNAIRE: AFRICAN-AMERICAN MANAGERS (AAM) IN CORPORATE MANAGEMENT

The questions below request specific information for the research. It will be highly appreciated that you complete the entire questionnaire. However, if there is any question that you do not feel confortable answering, please feel free to leave it blank.

Position held _____ Sex ( )_____

Level of Education _____

Years of Experience ( ) _____

SECTION I: GENERAL INFORMATION

1. Type of organization:
   _____ Industry   _____ Commerce   _____ Service

2. Number of employees in your firm:
   _____ AAM   _____ White Manager (WM)   _____ Total

3. Organization's foundation date:

4. Please, describe your organization's managers.

Title	Sex	AAM	WM
General Manager or President			
Vice-President or Division Manager			
Production Manager			
Human Resource Manager			
Materials Manager			
Q. A. Manager			
Market Manager			
Comptroller			
Other (please, add to the list):			

5. Do you have an Affirmative Action Program or any similar equal opportunity outreach program (incentive) for furthering the use of African-Americans in management?
   _____ Yes   _____ No

Section II: Perceptions

Please, select the number of alternatives that best describe your point of view regarding the next item (5 = Strongly agree, 4 = Fairly agree, 3 - Do not agree, 2 = Strongly disagree, 1 = Do not know)

	5	4	3	2	1
6. My firm's needs require academic qualifications that are present in AAN.	___	___	___	___	___
7. AAM are qualified academically but exhibit a lack of other need attributes to become good managers.	___	___	___	___	___
8. Inappropriate education is hindering AAM's access to managerial positions.	___	___	___	___	___
9. AAM obtained their experience in management in previous jobs.	___	___	___	___	___
10. AAM obtained their experience in management through "in house" training.	___	___	___	___	___
11. AAM that you know are part of a professional network inside or outside their organization.	___	___	___	___	___
12. Most professional AAM are competing among themselves unnecessarily.	___	___	___	___	___
13. Most professional AAM that you know are supportive of each other.	___	___	___	___	___
14. Most professional AAM that you know are manipulative with each other.	___	___	___	___	___
15. Most professional AAM that you know are comprehensive toward each other.	___	___	___	___	___
16. Most professional AAM that you knows are apprehensive with other AAM.	___	___	___	___	___
17. Inappropriate professional networking is hindering AAMs access to managerial position.	___	___	___	___	___
18. AAM have to work harder than WM to attain the same status.	___	___	___	___	___

19. AAM's job opportunities are equal to WM.   ____ ____ ____ ____ ____

20. In order to be successful, AAM have to sacrifice more.   ____ ____ ____ ____ ____

21. In order to be successful, AAM have to sacrifice the family time.   ____ ____ ____ ____ ____

22. In order to be successful, AAM have to sacrifice the time spent with friends.   ____ ____ ____ ____ ____

23. In order to be successful, AAM have to sacrifice the time and involvement in leisure activities.   ____ ____ ____ ____ ____

24. Since AAM are recently entering into the work force, most of them have limited experience to qualify for a managerial position.   ____ ____ ____ ____ ____

25. When recruiting my organization's present managers, there were experienced AAM interested in this position.   ____ ____ ____ ____ ____

26. AAM can apply the same effort to their career as WM do.   ____ ____ ____ ____ ____

27. AAM are good managers because they have the same management style.   ____ ____ ____ ____ ____

28. WM prefer to work with WM because they have the same management style.   ____ ____ ____ ____ ____

29. African-Americans prefer to work with African Americans because they have the same management style.   ____ ____ ____ ____ ____

30.In your opinion, which of the following characteristics are promoting AAM in their career development?

Promotion of incentive mechanism   ____ ____ ____ ____ ____

Legal requirements and laws   ____ ____ ____ ____ ____

Increased number of educated AAM   ____ ____ ____ ____ ____

Career development programs   ____ ____ ____ ____ ____

Managing diversity techniques   ____ ____ ____ ____ ____

Awareness of management skills   ____ ____ ____ ____ ____

Corporate social responsibility   ____ ____ ____ ____ ____

Shortage of qualified AAM   ____ ____ ____ ____ ____

Other reasons: ____ ____ ____ ____ ____

31. In your opinion, which of the following characteristics are hindering AAM in their career development?

Lack of confidence   ____ ____ ____ ____ ____

Lack of emotional controls   ____ ____ ____ ____ ____

Difficult in handling pressure   ____ ____ ____ ____ ____

Excessively aggressive   ____ ____ ____ ____ ____

Lack of aggressiveness   ____ ____ ____ ____ ____

Lack of discipline   ____ ____ ____ ____ ____

Insufficient education   ____ ____ ____ ____ ____

Lack of technical & administrative skills   ____ ____ ____ ____ ____

Inadequate communication skills   ____ ____ ____ ____ ____

Insufficient human relation skills   ____ ____ ____ ____ ____

Lack of decision making skills   ____ ____ ____ ____ ____

Lack of time management skills   ____ ____ ____ ____ ____

Lack of experience   ____ ____ ____ ____ ____

Rivalry of WM and peers   ____ ____ ____ ____ ____

Jealousy of AAM and peers   ____ ____ ____ ____ ____

AAM's preference for traditional roles
as mediators, harmonizers, and pacifiers   ____ ____ ____ ____ ____

Aversion to relocate   ____ ____ ____ ____ ____

Do not want to work long hours
or unusual schedule   ____ ____ ____ ____ ____

Excessively outspoken   ____ ____ ____ ____ ____

Simply being an AAM   ____ ____ ____ ____ ____

Others (Please add to the list)   ____ ____ ____ ____ ____

SECTION III: EVALUATION

32. How satisfied are you with your managers?

	Extremely Satisfied	Very Satisfied	Somewhat Satisfied	Not at all Satisfied
WM	_____	_____	_____	_____
AAM	_____	_____	_____	_____

33. How do you rate AAM's productivity and job quality?
___ Equal to WM   ___ Inferior to WM   ___ Superior to WM

34. What is your opinion of AAM's managerial style?
___ It is the same as WM's managerial style. There are no differences.
___ It is very different from WMOs managerial style.
___ It is somewhat different to WM's managerial style.

35. In your opinion, in which managerial skills to AAM perform better? (Select one.)
___Technical skills   ___ Human Skills   ___ Conceptual

SECTION IV: FUTURE PLANS

36. How many AAM managerial positions do you think your firm will open in the near future?
___ Next year   ___ Next 2 to 3 years ___ In 4 to 5 years
37. If you need to decide among two individuals of different gender with the same qualifications, which one would you select?
___ AAM candidate   ___ WM candidate